Heaven & Other Plays

Heaven & Other Plays

by

David Edgecombe

**Eastern Caribbean Institute
Frederiksted, Virgin Islands**

This book is dedicated to my wife, Lenore

Contents

Foreword

I would be less than truthful if I told you it matters nothing that after some 20 years of writing plays, not one of these plays has been staged, to my knowledge, by a secondary school in the Caribbean, other than when I was a school boy and staged them myself.

No play of mine has ever been staged on any of the three campuses of the University of the West Indies, nor the University of Guyana, nor the College of the Bahamas. In fact, the only University that has staged any of my plays (two to date) is the University of the Virgin Islands.

No play of mine is on the Caribbean Examination Council (CXC) syllabus, and it bothers me.

So I asked a former teacher, who at the time was a high official in Montserrat's education system, why none of my plays is ever read, to say nothing of staged, in the schools? She said, jokingly, or at least with a big grin, that if my plays are as controversial and troublesome as I was when she taught me, I shouldn't be too surprised if nobody wishes to inflict them on impressionable young minds.

It was a diplomatic response. As a sixteen year old school boy I was dragged before the principal by another teacher, who accused me of attempting to take over the school. She was the staff advisor to the school's Dramatic Society and I its president. We had fought bitterly over what play should be offered that term. She insisted it should be one of the European classics. I argued it should be the West Indian play **Goose and Gander** by Wilfred Redhead. She pointed out how uplifting the classics were and how well they had established their value by "withstanding the test of time." I pointed out we were West Indians, and it was time we started staging our own plays. We ended up doing both plays. And although I don't remember exactly why she complained me to the principal, I always felt it had more to do with me insisting on staging the West Indian play than with anything else. In any case it was a mistake in those days to disagree with 'teacher' and I disagreed with too many of mine. It got me a bad reputation.

After I left school, I graduated from bane of teachers to bane of Chief Ministers. One former Chief Minister would seek a court injunction to stop a play of mine from being staged. One ruling Chief Minister would get an injunction, still in place, to stop me from writing unflattering articles about him, and would sue me for libel and win. Yet another soon-to-be Chief Minister would persuade the citizenry I was a mere playwright, an actor, a purveyor of fantasy whom all concerned citizens should disregard.

So, common sense, if not logic, dictates that if I'm objectionable, my plays must also be objectionable. No educator should be expected to advance the suicidal proposal that these plays be studied and performed in schools.

I understand this. Maybe would even accept it, as the wages of my sins, say, if it were the real reason my plays are not studied in schools. But it isn't. If it were, other Caribbean playwrights would be studied. But they aren't. In fact, there is at this moment not one Caribbean play listed in the syllabus of the Caribbean Examination Council (CXC). Not one secondary school student from Jamaica to Guyana is officially expected to read or see even one Caribbean play as part of his or her studies.

Surely, all Caribbean playwrights can't be objectionable. Surely our work ought not to be collectively offensive, except perhaps to those who regard Caribbean creative efforts generally as offensive. And, sadly, too many of those have been our own Caribbean people.

No. The problem is bigger than the individual playwright. Bigger than all the Caribbean playwrights put together. It is, in fact, the biggest problem every Caribbean playwright—without exception—has faced and will continue to face in the foreseeable future. Simply put, it is this: there isn't and never was a vibrant Caribbean theater.

There is of course an inherent danger in attempting a simple explanation of such a complex matter. A simple answer is likely to be dismissed as simplistic or, even worse, untrue. What, for example, does the absence of a vibrant Caribbean theater have to do with the absence of Caribbean plays from Caribbean schoolrooms? Where is the connection? Also, how can you say there's no vibrant Caribbean Theater when each year many Caribbean plays are staged in Jamaica and the rest of the Caribbean, and in the U.S., Canada, and England?

There are indeed some fine theater groups in the Caribbean which, under difficult circumstances, perform a wide range of plays, some of which are by Caribbean playwrights. It is good to note that there are groups in the United States, Canada and England which produce Caribbean plays. I salute all those who have written even one Caribbean play. I have the highest respect and regard for that handful of playwrights who continue to write plays although there is so little inducement and support for an activity that is going to net them more frustration than anything else.

But all of this does not a vibrant Caribbean Theater make.

About a year before he died in 1991, I asked the Caribbean playwright, poet, director and teacher Dennis Scott, when would Caribbean Theater ever come into its own? In other words when would we see the vibrant Caribbean Theater so many of us have dreamed of? He thought about it briefly and said: "When the Caribbean playwrights get out of politics, (a dig at me, who had just run unsuccessfully for a seat in Montserrat's legislature,) come home from wherever they are teaching and get back to writing and producing plays in the Caribbean."

It was a good answer in that it focused on the importance of the playwright in the creation of any kind of theater. The role of the playwright is not always understood or appreciated, even sometimes by those involved in theater. This was never more evident than at that historic Caribbean Playwrights Conference in 1981, whose stated purpose was to produce better Caribbean plays and hence a better Caribbean theater. Right in the middle of this exercise which had raised the hopes of Caribbean Theater to unprecedented heights, the question was posed: why a playwrights' conference? Why is so much effort, time and money being expended on them? It was proposed that what we really need are actors and directors happily engaged in street theater. People who can assemble under any mango tree or street light and just create theater from anything or nothing. I'm happy to note that some of the more ferocious pushers of this heresy have since tried their hands at writing plays. I hope the effort has also brought a greater understanding of the pivotal role of the playwright in the quest for a vibrant Caribbean Theater.

Derek Walcott, winner of the 1992 Nobel Prize for Literature, stated what needs to happen for Caribbean Theater to come into its own in his 1970 essay *What the Twilight Says: An Overture*, which appears as an introduction to *Dream On Monkey Mountain and Other Plays*, (Farrar, Straus and Giroux.) "When one began twenty years ago," he wrote, "it was in the faith that one was creating not merely a play, but a theater, and not merely a theater, but its environment." For there to be a vibrant Caribbean Theater, for it to come into its own, and flourish, a way must be found to create this 'environment' which will nourish and sustain it.

A Caribbean theater needs first of all to be distinctly and

uncompromisingly Caribbean. It needs to tell the story of Caribbean people, their history and their heritage, their pains, their joys, their hopes. It must foster and encourage playwrights. Allow for the development of Caribbean plays through workshops, performances, dramaturgy, criticism. Allow for first-class productions of these plays. Allow for experimentation. Allow for comprehensive distribution of these plays as books, videos, films and audio recordings. And, of signal importance, it must afford those involved in it the opportunity to earn a decent livelihood from practicing their crafts. All of this cannot happen without that sustaining network, that 'environment' which is yet to be created.

And I am saying nothing new. Nothing that Caribbean playwrights, and dramatists generally, haven't recognised for a long time. It is clearly this recognition which drove Errol Hill in his early pioneering days of trying to forge a Caribbean Theater. (It is my view, incidentally, that Mr. Hill ought to be regarded as the father of contemporary Caribbean Theater for his exemplary work in the 40's, 50's and 60's.) It is this recognition which led the University of the West Indies Extra-Mural Department to publish and disseminate that most influential collection of plays that has come to be known as the Red & White series; to have held drama workshops around the region; to have sent people like Hill, Noel Vaz, Dennis Scott and Daphne Hacket to so many islands to help fledging theater groups by teaching them the arts and crafts of theater. It is this recognition which led to the formation of such groups in the 70's as Theater Information Exchange (TIE) and The Caribbean United States Theater Exchange (CARIBUSTE). It is this recognition which led to the TIE/CARIBUSTE Caribbean Playwrights' Conference at the University of the Virgin Islands, St. Thomas, in 1981 and to the formation of such organizations as

The Association of Caribbean Theater Artists (ACTRA) and the Eastern Caribbean Popular Theater Organization (ECPTO) in the 80's. All of these movements have been pan-Caribbean in perspective, and rightly so.

But it is one thing to recognize a goal and another thing altogether to achieve it. The dramatists have tried, continue to try, and will never stop trying. This is particularly true of the playwright. An actor may feel that the pinnacle of success is to play Hamlet, and having done so can die in peace. Or a director will speak with reverence and pride about directing Beckett or Brecht, feeling no doubt, that there's greater merit to this than directing Walcott or Trevor Rhone. But the playwright knows in his bones, that, irrespective of what generous accommodations are afforded him in other peoples' theaters, without his own Caribbean theater he is a homeless wanderer. This is why the playwright, more than anyone else, wishes to see the establishment of a vibrant Caribbean Theater.

It is no accident that almost the first thing Walcott did on winning his prize of close to U.S. $1,000,000, was to announce his renewed support for the Trinidad Theater Workshop. He can no more abandon his dream of a vibrant Caribbean Theater, complete with the environment to sustain it, than he can stop himself from being, at one and the same time, both observer and participant in the game of life.

What can we learn from past efforts to establish a vibrant Caribbean theater? Errol Hill and the Extra Mural Department of the University of the West Indies were on the right track with their early programs in drama. Mr. Hill and his colleagues decided to write plays and to encourage the writing of plays; to teach theater skills, which up to today are still sadly lacking throughout the English-speaking Caribbean; to help with the performance and development of these plays; to publish and distribute these plays throughout the Caribbean. The value of this initiative cannot be too highly rated. It resulted in that collection of plays published by the University of the West Indies in the 1960's: The Red and White Series, made up of one-act plays; the Yellow and White Series, made up of medium length plays; and the Blue and White Series, made of full-length plays.

It is unfortunate that younger dramatists, like myself, came eventually to reject this entire series, even though it served the good purpose of providing Caribbean Plays for us to perform when no other Caribbean plays could be found.

This rejection is perhaps both understandable and justifiable, but no less unfortunate. Walcott writing in the essay cited earlier said: *"the sparse body of West Indian theater still feeds on the subject of emaciation and what it produces, rogues, drunkards, mad men, outcasts, and sets against this the pastoral of the peasant. Its comedy begins with the premise that all are starved or deprived, or defend themselves from being further deprived by threats."* He stated further: *"the people like the actors awaited language. They confronted a variety of styles and masks, but because they were casual about commitment, ashamed of their speech, they were moved only by the tragi-comic, and facial..."* [Walcott, 1970]

It was natural for young playwrights to want to craft plays which said and did more than those they had grown up on. They wanted to be able to present other aspects of Caribbean life, to bring into existence a more dynamic theater. This is healthy, but in attempting to do it the older plays got shunned. Too often in the Caribbean we behave as if the only way we can build, is to destroy. The result is that we are forever re-inventing the wheel, instead of using the wheels which already exist to move us to higher ground. I would advocate a re-examination of these plays, a re-assessment of them. And some were very good. I think particularly of Hill's **Dance Bongo**, an extremely well crafted, well written play, which makes exciting theater.

Another unfortunate occurrence is that in our zeal to be relevant, to be politically and ideologically correct, we frequently failed to pay enough attention to good craftsmanship. As a result we turned out, and continue to turn out, some pretty bad plays.

Which brings me to an important point. In a vibrant Caribbean Theater, standards of excellence need to be set and maintained. How are these standards to be set? What would be a good Caribbean play? How would it differ from a good play—period?

Over the years I've heard many different views, some of which border on dogma. There are those who hold that for a play to be authentically Caribbean it must contain drumming and dance. Others hold that it must be in dialect. Still others hold that plays with a 'story line' with the classic beginning, middle and end are passé. Only the abstract, the avant-garde, the work with no linear development is of merit.

I mistrust dogma and believe the artist must be allowed his subject and treatment. Playmaking as well as storytelling are ancient, universal art forms. It can only help us to study the best of these from around the world and use them as a standard against which to measure our own efforts. In other words it would be foolish not to recognise that we play in a world arena and to set our standards accordingly.

The Caribbean must be one of the few places left on earth which perpetuates the anomaly of learning and producing other people's plays, indeed other people's literature, ahead of its own. But, strange as it may seem, the term Caribbean Literature does not even include Caribbean drama. It means

Caribbean poetry and fiction but rarely, if ever, Caribbean drama.

Let me illustrate. The University of Miami started a Caribbean Writers' Seminar in August 1991. Since then Edward 'Kamu' Brathwaithe has taught poetry and George Lamming fiction. No seminar has yet been offered in drama. Again, when I was a student at Concordia University, Montreal, from 1980 to '82, it was possible to take a few courses in Caribbean Literature. You could study West Indian novels and short stories. You could study West Indian poems and poets. But you could not study West Indian drama. There were simply no courses in Caribbean Theater or in Caribbean plays. The closest you could get to it was a study of some of Derek Walcott's plays, **Dream On Monkey Mountain** particularly, as part of your study of his poetry. In 1985 I spent 6 weeks touring the United States with a group of writers from Latin America. As part of our program we met several publishers in several cities. They showed considerable interest in publishing fiction and prose, less in publishing poetry and absolutely none in publishing plays. One publisher said to me: "The truth is there's just no market that I know of for Caribbean plays." Most revealing is that in awarding Walcott the Nobel Prize for literature, no mention was made of the fact that he is a playwright, nor of any of his books of plays. And as I've said already there is presently no Caribbean play on the CXC syllabus. Drama is not regarded as part of Caribbean Literature, or at least, not an important part.

Part of my contention is that a vibrant Caribbean theater can help to change this for the benefit of all Caribbean Literature. It should come as no surprise that the two Caribbean plays (**An Echo in The Bone** by Dennis Scott and **Old Story Time** by Trevor Rhone) placed on the CXC syllabus for

1995 are both from Jamaica which boasts the closest thing to a vibrant Caribbean Theater. Few Caribbean people read Caribbean fiction and less read any kind of poetry. A vibrant theater can help bring these works to life and make them accessible to more people, as happened with Erna Brodber's ***Jane and Louisa Will Soon Come Home***, Earl Lovelace's ***Wine of Astonishment*** and Kamu Brathwaite's ***Mother Poem***.

Also, a vibrant theater is perhaps our best defense against cultural imperialism, which has grown a thousand times more powerful with the spread of cable TV. I suspect the effects of this could be even more devastating than slavery was if steps are not taken to counter it. More than ever a vibrant Caribbean theater is needed. Right now we should be actively writing and producing plays, not just for the stage but for film and television.

Just the other day I realized with a start that my confidence in my abilities to change the world has diminished. It is partly out of this realization that I present this book with three of my plays: ***Heaven, Making It,*** and ***For Better For Worse***. I want to add them to that 'sparse body' of Caribbean plays, easily available for production. My hope is that this publication will lead to a much greater audience for the plays. I want it to be available to companies looking for Caribbean plays to produce. I want it to make its way into our schools and universities. I particularly want it in the hands of young people with a passion to produce plays about themselves.

And I have a selfish reason for this. I fear it will fall to a new generation of dramatists, with better communication and organizational skills, a greater sense of purpose, more money—whatever—to make real the age old dream of Caribbean playwrights for a vibrant Caribbean Theater.

David Edgecombe
St. Thomas, USVI
March, 1993.

David Edgecombe

Heaven
and Other Plays

Heaven

Heaven was first performed by the University of the Virgin Islands Theater at the Little Theatre, St. Thomas on April 19, 1991. It then went on tour to St. Maarten, St. Kitts, Antigua, and Montserrat. The play was designed and directed by Dennis Parker with the following cast:

WAYNE	Neal Richardson
CYNTHIA	Lavida Thomas
SAM	Norwell Donovan
TONY	Seymour Davis
DILYS	Roxanne Martin

Following the tour ***Heaven*** was re-written and re-staged on August 30, 1991, at the Reichhold Center for the Arts, St. Thomas, with the following cast:

WAYNE	Neal Richardson
CYNTHIA	Lavida Thomas
SAM	Hans Eisler
TONY	Jerome Kendall
DILYS	Myrenna Ogbu McGriff

This version of the play, which appears here with further small changes, was directed by the author and designed by Dennis Parker.

Characters

WAYNE, a school boy, about 17

CYNTHIA, a civil servant, 18 or 19

SAM, a businessman in his 60s

TONY, a lawyer, early 40s

DILYS, Tony's wife, 35

Setting

The annex, back yard or back patio of a discotheque called Heaven. Two round tables—one stage left, the other stage right—each with two chairs. A door leading to Heaven, up left. A door to a bathroom, right of center. Another 'exit', down left, leading to an open field or park (which does not have to be shown).

The whole play takes place here, one Saturday night.

ACT ONE

As the lights come up, Wayne and Cynthia are rehearsing a dance without music. They go through the sequence with Wayne counting out the steps.

WAYNE: Great! That's it! That's it! You got it! Alright, next section now. Follow me.

[He shows her some steps. She tries to follow but fails]

CYNTHIA: Man, this is too hard.

WAYNE: Easy. Let's try it again. After three. And a one and a two and a...

[They dance. She is hesitant and uncertain and misses her step]

CYNTHIA: Look, I just can't get it right.

WAYNE: Concentrate, okay, just concentrate.

CYNTHIA: It's too hard, man.

WAYNE: You almost have it. Once we run it few more times we'll be all set.

CYNTHIA: A few more times? You no see how me tired?

WAYNE: Stop complaining and let's go from the top.

CYNTHIA: What I'm trying to tell you, Wayne, is that I can't get the steps. I don't know what I'm doing.

WAYNE: Alright. I'll show you again. Just follow me. Come on, just follow me.

CYNTHIA: *[Reluctantly getting into place behind him]* Okay, Mr. Choreographer, show me.

WAYNE: Concentrate. After four. And one, two, three, four. And...

     [He demonstrates and she follows]

WAYNE: How's that?

CYNTHIA: Good, so far.

WAYNE: Alright, let's try it together. *[They dance and she misses her step again]*

CYNTHIA: I give up.

WAYNE: Don't. Come back and let's run through it again.

CYNTHIA: Either you come up with something simpler or let's forget it.

WAYNE: Let's try it one more time.

CYNTHIA: Let's try something simpler.

WAYNE: But this is perfect, Cynthia. It's just right. We can win with it.

CYNTHIA: But I can't get the steps right. That's what I'm trying to tell you.

WAYNE: If you had come to rehearsals you wouldn't be having this problem now.

CYNTHIA: I'm not having no problem. You're making it a problem. I say let's forget the damn contest and just enjoy ourselves tonight.

WAYNE: I asked you to dance with me, Cynthia. I asked you because I believe I could depend on you.

CYNTHIA: I thought you asked me because of my spectacular talent.

WAYNE: It's just a big joke to you, right?

CYNTHIA: No, it's killing me and that's no joke.

WAYNE: We agreed to rehearse three times. Twice you don't even show up. The third time you reach almost two hours late, and wouldn't even make an effort to get it right.

CYNTHIA: It's not that I'm not making an effort. I just didn't expect you to have something so complicated.

WAYNE: It only seem complicated because you haven't practiced.

CYNTHIA: Look, Wayne, this week was nothing but hell, so just back off, okay?

WAYNE: A lot of good dancers are in the competition tonight. We can't come with any ole stupidness and hope to win.

CYNTHIA: So let's just go in for the hell of it and have some fun.

WAYNE: I need to win! *[Pause]* I need the money.

CYNTHIA: What money? A hundred, hundred and fifty dollars?

WAYNE: A hundred each if we win. When we win.

CYNTHIA: That's money to be breaking your ass like this for?

WAYNE: Stop bitching, okay? It might not be much but it will help pay for books and school leaving exams next term. Every bit helps.

CYNTHIA: You don't need to explain it to me, Wayne. Come let's run the dance.

WAYNE: From the top?

CYNTHIA: From the top.

WAYNE: With the music?

CYNTHIA: Yeah, let's try it with the music.

WAYNE: Get ready.

             [Wayne turns on a cassette player and they run the dance from the top. While they dance, Sam enters and watches them. At the end, he applauds]

SAM: Fantastic!

WAYNE: You like it, Mr. Drummonds?

SAM: Out of this world.

WAYNE: Looks good?

SAM: Better than good. Fabulous.

WAYNE: You see. I told you we could do it.

CYNTHIA: We haven't done it yet.

WAYNE: But, we will. Dance like that tonight and we must win the two hundred bucks.

CYNTHIA: Stop counting your chickens. What about all those good dancers competing tonight?

WAYNE: Can't touch us. Not one of them. Me and you are the best. THE BEST! Just keep telling yourself that.

SAM: Look, ley me buy you both something to drink.
             After that performance you must be thirsty. What
             you having, Wayne?

WAYNE: Coke is good.

SAM: Yeah?

WAYNE: You know, ice cold and refreshing, in bottle or
             can.

SAM: Oh, you had me fooled there for a minute. And you
             Miss...What's it again?

CYNTHIA: Corbette.

SAM: Yes, of course. What would you like?

CYNTHIA: I'll have a beer.

WAYNE: Beer?

CYNTHIA: Don't worry. I am not going to get high and forget
             my steps.

WAYNE: Forget the beer. Bring her a Coke or a juice, sir.

CYNTHIA: I want a beer.

WAYNE: Have your beer after the contest.

CYNTHIA: Wayne, I want a beer and I am going to have a beer.
             Now. *[Pause]*

SAM: That settles it? Good. One Coke and one beer in
             a minute. I'll be right back. *[He starts to leave but
             turns back]* Tell you what, Wayne. You must know
             your way around this...Heaven better than I ever
             would, so why not do the honors?

WAYNE: If you like.

SAM: *[Giving Wayne money from a wad of bills]* You're
              the one with all the youth and energy, anyway.

WAYNE: A hundred dollars? You don't have anything
              smaller, sir?

SAM: Bigger, maybe. Smaller, no.

WAYNE: Anything for you, sir?

SAM: Brandy straight up.

WAYNE: Coming right up.

SAM: And, Wayne, make sure it's the best they have in
              the house. Double.

WAYNE: Nothing but the finest for you, Mr. Drummonds.
              [Wayne exits]

SAM: Clearly you were born to dance.

CYNTHIA: You really liked it?

SAM: Loved it. If there's a better dancer than you, she's
              not on earth. Or in Heaven for that matter.

CYNTHIA: I hope not in Heaven. I really want us to win
              tonight, for Wayne's sake. The ole jackass.

SAM: What?

CYNTHIA: Never mind me. It's just that he gets me so mad
              sometimes.

SAM: Don't let him get you mad. Don't let anything get
              you mad.

CYNTHIA: Ever?

SAM: Let's start with tonight and build from there.
              Tonight I don't want you to be mad. I want you to
              be happy.

CYNTHIA: I want to be happy too.

SAM: I want to make you happy.

CYNTHIA: Is that so?

SAM: One hundred percent so.

CYNTHIA: Why are all you men like that?

SAM: Like what?

CYNTHIA: "Forget the beer!" He's not even a man yet. Not
             even out of school, and he wants to pitch orders
             to a big woman like me.

SAM: You don't look any older than him to me.

CYNTHIA: I'm a year older. Plus he's still in school and I'm
             out working for my own money.

SAM: How come?

CYNTHIA: How come what?

SAM: You're out of school?

CYNTHIA: You don't know?

SAM: Haven't a clue.

CYNTHIA: Then you must be the only one.

SAM: What happened?

CYNTHIA: You don't know, you don't know.

SAM: I'd really like to know, so tell me.

CYNTHIA: No way. I'm supposed to be happy tonight, re-
             member?

SAM: Yes, of course. Well, where were we? Oh, yes, Wayne giving you orders. Look at the bright side. Ten, maybe even five years ago you would have been happy to obey.

CYNTHIA: Me? Not me. Not ten years ago, not fifty, not ever.

SAM: It wouldn't even have occurred to you to do anything other than obey.

CYNTHIA: Never happen. Not me. Me, Cynthia Corbette? Never happen.

SAM: Hot blooded and rebellious, eh.

CYNTHIA: That's me. I'm not putting up with no crap from nobody. Not again.

SAM: Not again?

CYNTHIA: Never mind.

SAM: Was that your boyfriend?

CYNTHIA: What?

SAM: Wayne is your boyfriend?

CYNTHIA: It look so?

SAM: Yeah, it look so to me.

CYNTHIA: Good.

SAM: But, being a man who knows that too many things are not what they appear to be, my question still stands. Is Wayne your boyfriend?

CYNTHIA: Suppose I tell you no?

SAM: So we're going to play games, then? Alright, if you say no, is no.

CYNTHIA: And suppose I say yes?

SAM: That I'll sooner believe.

CYNTHIA: And what difference would it make?

SAM: Okay, let me put it another way: Do you have a boy friend?

CYNTHIA: That's for me to know and for you to find out.

SAM: Oh, God!

CYNTHIA: Oh, God, what?

SAM: I thought that line was long dead and buried. I never expected to hear that one, and especially not from you.

CYNTHIA: Well, you just heard it.

SAM: And I'm very disappointed. Grossly disappointed.

CYNTHIA: That's your ass. Be disappointed all you want.

SAM: Look, forget I asked.

CYNTHIA: I'm going to look for Wayne.

SAM: He'll soon be back, I'm sure.

CYNTHIA: He's taking too long.

SAM: Relax. What's the hurry?

CYNTHIA: I want to go look for him.

SAM: Yes, of course. Please go and see what's holding up your boyfriend. Make sure no other woman is stealing him away.

CYNTHIA: Wayne just likes me, that's all. Okay?

SAM: I wouldn't hold that against him.

CYNTHIA: And I like him too. A hell of a lot.

SAM: You just don't like him giving you orders, right?

CYNTHIA: Aaah! That's nothing. I know how to deal with that. He's my best friend and I want to help him win tonight.

SAM: Good luck, although I don't see how you can lose.

CYNTHIA: What you doing here, anyway?

SAM: I want to be in the company of angels.

CYNTHIA: You don't look like a disco person to me. And, come to think of it, I don't remember ever seeing you here.

SAM: One angel in particular.

CYNTHIA: Oh?

SAM: You.

CYNTHIA: Oh, really? *[She laughs derisively]*

SAM: You think it's funny?

CYNTHIA: Well, no. Not really.

SAM: So why the laugh?

CYNTHIA: Really, Mr. Drummonds. What would you be wanting with a little girl like me?

SAM: To make you happy, that's all. Ahh, I almost forgot. And to help make it possible for you to enjoy yourself, I brought you this. *[He gives her an envelope]*

CYNTHIA: What is it?

SAM: Look and see. Open it. Look at it. *[Wayne enters]*

CYNTHIA: Finally.

SAM: But…let's keep this between the two of us. Okay?

CYNTHIA: Alright.

SAM: Put it away and we'll speak about it later.

CYNTHIA: *[To Wayne]* What took you so long?

WAYNE: You should see the crowd inside. *[Passing drinks]* Here you go, Mr. Drummonds. Here you go…partner. And here's the change.

SAM: Keep it.

WAYNE: Seriously?

SAM: Well, you worked didn't you?

WAYNE: Worked?

SAM: You went for the drinks.

WAYNE: Naah, man, that's not work. I was glad to do that for you, Mr. Drummonds. *[He tries to give back the money]*

SAM: Never say no to money, Wayne. Even if you think I'm a fool to give it to you, let that be my problem. Keep it. You deserve it for doing such a great job on the dance.

WAYNE: Thank you, sir. Thank you very, very much.

SAM: I used to be quite a dancer myself, you know.

WAYNE: Have any good steps you want to show me?

SAM: You bet I do. *[He does a little fancy foot-work]* Twinkle-toes they used to call me. I don't get to do much of it anymore, but I still love to see good dancing. Cheers. To your success.

            [They all drink]

CYNTHIA: Hey, this is not beer!

WAYNE: I said you're not to drink any beer. No beer.

CYNTHIA: I don't believe this crap.

WAYNE: Time enough for beer after we win.

CYNTHIA: Don' skylark with me, you know, Wayne. Don' skylark wid me at all.

WAYNE: Do it for me. Okay. For me.

CYNTHIA: You know what I should do for you? Take this drink and throw it over your damn head. That's what I should do for you.

WAYNE: Hey, have some respect for Mr. Drummonds.

CYNTHIA: Go back for me beer, Wayne, or ley me go for it meself.

WAYNE: All joke aside, Cynthia, it will make me feel better if you don't drink. More confident.

CYNTHIA: One little beer?

WAYNE: Yeah, one little beer. *[Pause]* For me, okay? Please. Please?

CYNTHIA: I don' know why I let you manipulate me like this, you know. *[She drinks]* Coke. A big woman like me on a Saturday night in Heaven drinking Coke.

SAM: Would you prefer milk and honey?

CYNTHIA: Ugh!

SAM: You have something against milk and honey?

CYNTHIA: Never tried it and probably never will. *[She laughs]*

SAM: Not planning to go to Heaven, then?

CYNTHIA: Don' make plans. Besides this Heaven here is the
            only one I intend to go to for a long, long time. *[She
            drinks]* Coke. I let you get away with murder, you
            know, Wayne Cabey, and I shouldn't.

WAYNE: *[Putting his head right next to hers]* Blame it on my
            irresistible charm and persuasive personality.

CYNTHIA: *[With mock seriousness, she threatens him with
            her drink]* Boy, move out me face before I dowse
            you with this stupid drink, eh.

WAYNE: Try.

CYNTHIA: Don' bet me, you know, Wayne.

WAYNE: Come on try. *[She feigns a couple of times]* You
            couldn't do it for a million dollars.

CYNTHIA: Smart ass. *[She throws the drink at him. He ducks
            under it and grabs her from behind. Playfully he
            kisses her on the cheek, lifts her up, twirls her,
            kisses the other cheek]* Put me down! Wayne, stop
            it! Put me down. *[He continues. Tony enters]* Put
            me down.

TONY: Hey, leave the girl alone.

WAYNE: Piss off! *[To Cynthia]* Come, let's go get you back
            your drink. *[He carries her in his arms towards the
            exit]*

TONY: *[Putting his hand on Wayne's shoulder]* I said to
            leave her alone.

WAYNE: Take your paws off me, man! *[Tony applies pressure to the shoulder. Wayne screams in pain and releases Cynthia]*

CYNTHIA: What you do that for? *[To Wayne]* You okay, Wayne? You alright? *[He nods]* What you hurt the boy for?

TONY: Who can't hear will feel...

CYNTHIA: You had no right, man.

TONY: ...If he paid more attention to his teacher, his Sunday School teacher and his mama he would know that. Then, maybe, he wouldn't have to get hurt.

CYNTHIA: Piss off, Tony Thompson. You hear me? Just piss off.

TONY: *[To Sam]* See what the world has come to? In the olden days, you helped a damsel in distress, she would hug you and kiss you and love you forever. Today, she cuss you. And you lucky if on top of that she don' turn around and kick you too.

CYNTHIA: You don' know how much I would just love to kick your ass in truth.

TONY: See?

CYNTHIA: Come on, Wayne, let's go. *[To Tony]:* Bully! *[They exit]*

SAM: Hot little number, that one.

TONY: You're telling me.

SAM: Great dancer too.

TONY: So I hear.

SAM: Hear? You're a man who's supposed to know these things.

TONY: Not any more. I'm keeping far from these young girls, nowadays. Leaving them all to you.

SAM: Bless your kind heart.

TONY: Once upon a time women used to be in love, but not any more. Today they all in business.

SAM: You ain't lying with that one.

TONY: Only a man like you could afford them, now.

SAM: I used to think so, but I'm not so sure anymore. The other night I took a pretty one out to dinner. First time I'm taking her out and check this. She takes one sip of her soup and says to me: you know, the problem with all the younger men today? They only interested in one thing: sex.

TONY: You didn't tell her it's the problem with all the older men too?

SAM: No, man. She knows sex could only be in our heads.

TONY: A bright girl.

SAM: Too bright. She tells me there's this young man who has an interest in her. Always bothering her up, always wanting to take her out, always telling her if she ever has any difficulties he's there waiting and ready to help her. So she eventually agrees to go out with him and tells him about this small problem she has. Nothing serious, mark you. All she needs to make it disappear is an urgent $4,000.

TONY: $4,000?

SAM: Wait, nuh. The guy says: no problem...

TONY: That must have been you, Sam.

SAM: Hold on, man. Pretty you know, my friend. Like the morning sun. And an actress. She puts those big, innocent eyes on me and there're tears in her voice: 'No problem' he says. 'No problem, haaa! He took me home and I never saw or heard from him again'.

TONY: So you wrote her a check?

SAM: Almost. I swear to God she almost had me. So much so in fact that I had to see how fast I could get her home too. And I must confess she's yet to see me or hear from me since then as well.

TONY: Come on, Sam. A little $4,000 would have made her happy and she in turn might have made you happy beyond your wildest dreams.

SAM: Might have. That's the operative word, my friend, might.

TONY: You don't take a chance you can't win.

SAM: Four thousand smakeroos! And that's just for openers. Well, when the stakes get so high I leave the game up to powerful lawyers like you.

TONY: I'm out of the game long before that, man.

SAM: The big problem is though, you can't really stay out of the game. Unless you're dead, of course.

TONY: And I take it you're not dead?

SAM: Well, you never know, considering I'm in Heaven tonight.

TONY: This Heaven is not for dead people, believe me.

SAM: But then you don't get to Heaven till you rise
            again. So maybe there's hope. Hell, they'd better
            be hope in Heaven. *[Pause]*

TONY: So, how's business?

SAM: As they say, a lot like sex. When it's good it's
            wonderful. When it's not good, it's still great. *[They
            both laugh]* How're things with you?

TONY: I'm thankful.

SAM: You should be, the way your cup runneth over.

TONY: You think my cup is running over, eh?

SAM: School children in Swaziland know your cup is
            running over.

TONY: And how come I doan know?

SAM: Don't be shy about it, my friend. Rather a cup
            running over any day than an empty one.

TONY: You should know.

SAM: You got that right. I've had it both ways and
            believe me, running over is best.

TONY: I'll drink to that. Shall we?

SAM: Definitely.

TONY: Drinks are inside.

SAM: The music inside is too loud for me. Tell you what,
            you run along and have your drink. I'll join you
            latter.

TONY: Come ahead, man.

SAM: Later. I want to stay here and enjoy the fresh air
            a bit longer.

TONY: Alone?

SAM: As you can see.

TONY: Something tells me you're on a mission tonight.

SAM: Of course I'm on a mission. A change of pace mission...a little relaxation mission.

TONY: That's it.

SAM: What else?

TONY: Well, as you know, us lawyers don't make good believers. Something tells me you're up to more than that.

SAM: I'd love to be. I want to be. Everybody always saying how great Heaven is and now I come to see for myself not an angel to be found.

TONY: You want to see angels come inside where the action is. This is just a sort of annex, if you need some fresh air and a little more privacy. This door leads to a bathroom. Out this way, is an open field with a few benches if you need even more...fresh air. *[He laughs]* Come, let's go get a drink and see what the angels look like.

             [Dilys enters]

DILYS: How you reach all the way out here already? I just turn my back for one minute and off you go leaving me all by myself.

TONY: My Darling, come say good night to a great man. And the sole reason for my apparent inattentiveness.

DILYS: Sam Drummonds? My dear cousin Sam. Well, well, well. Hi, Sam. I didn't know you went to places like this.

SAM: *[Kissing her cheek]* So what am I? The devil?

DILYS: Don't forget he used to be in Heaven too.

SAM: True. And you know, one of the main reasons I
              never came to this place before is the name?

DILYS: Heaven?

SAM: That's right. They should never have called it that.

DILYS: You're putting me on.

SAM: Dead serious.

DILYS: Did you and Tony discuss this?

SAM: Not that I remember.

DILYS: You must have.

SAM: Did we?

DILYS: He used to always say the same thing.

TONY: Great minds don't have to discuss things to come
              to the same conclusions.

DILYS: Tony, yes. But I never figured you for getting upset
              with something like this, Sam.

TONY: People have to be sensitive about such things.

SAM: Exactly.

DILYS: Oh, please, a name is just a name.

SAM: You wouldn't call your dog Jesus, would you?

DILYS: Why not? My dog. Or my son.

SAM: Jesus.

DILYS: That's if I can get my husband to agree, of course.

TONY: And you know I'll never agree to any such thing.
              [He exits to bathroom]

SAM: Thank God for that.

DILYS: I know you're putting me on, Sam. You have to be.
              What the hell. It's just a name. Jesus, Heaven, big
              deal.

SAM: It's not that I'm a saint, mark you…

DILYS: Precisely.

SAM: I'm not even particularly devout. But I think
              certain things should always be kept sacred.
              Names like Jesus and Heaven.

DILYS: Oh, stop it.

              [Wayne enters]

WAYNE: Please excuse me, Mr. Drummonds, did Cynthia
              come back out here?

SAM: Haven't seen her, son.

WAYNE: Okay, thank you. *[He crosses to the area where
              they rehearsed the dance]*

DILYS: Let me ask this young man what he thinks. Tell
              me something, what you think of the name
              Heaven?

              [Tony returns]

WAYNE: What's there to think?

DILYS: As a name for this discotheque?

WAYNE: Most appropriate.

SAM: How's that?

WAYNE: Well, it's a place where people come to be happy, isn't it?

DILYS: But of course. You're young enough to see that, but these two guys are over the hills and not with it. Maybe you could teach them something.

WAYNE: But it could also be hell for some people.

SAM: Is that right?

WAYNE: Well, you know...some people drink too much sometimes, or smoke-up too much. Others get their girls taken away from them. Some men leave their wives at home to come in here and frolic with women half their wife's age. That I imagine must be hell for the wives.

DILYS: A most perceptive young man. What's your name?

WAYNE: Wayne. Wayne Cabey.

DILYS: You're in the competition tonight?

WAYNE: Yes.

DILYS: Then I must certainly keep an eye out for you. Good luck. And thanks.

WAYNE: Any time.

DILYS: Well, like it or not, Sam, you're in Heaven. So loosen up. Relax. Take off your tie. You'll have a better time. Come, let me fix you up. *[She takes off his tie. Opens the front of his shirt and breaks the shirt collar over the jacket]* There. That's better.

SAM: Whatever you say. I don't agree with you and the name, but in such matters I trust your judgement implicitly.

DILYS: Actually you chose a good night to come. We're celebrating our tenth anniversary tonight. Did Tony tell you?

SAM: Er...yes, of course. He was just dragging me inside for a celebration drink.

DILYS: Maybe we should celebrate out here instead, with all the confusion inside. Eh, darling?

TONY: Whatever makes you happy, honey.

DILYS: *[To Wayne]* My husband and I are celebrating our tenth anniversary tonight. Would you have a glass of champagne with us?

WAYNE: Thanks, but I don't drink.

TONY: Tell you what, let's go inside, see if we can get my friend here hooked up with somebody and then we can all come back out later.

SAM: Sounds good to me. *[They begin to leave]* Look, you two go ahead. I'll pop in here, *[indicates bathroom]* do what you can't do for me, and join you in a minute.

[They leave. Wayne rehearses dance movements. Sam returns from john]

Lost your dance partner, eh?

WAYNE: She'll be here, sir.

SAM: How long you worked on that dance?

WAYNE: Just tonight.

SAM: You been dancing together long?

WAYNE: All through school.

SAM: She's still in school?

WAYNE: No. She had to leave.

SAM: Had to leave? How come?

WAYNE: Well...er...I'm not a good person to ask, sir.

SAM: Surely, whatever it is, you can tell me.

WAYNE: I wish I could, sir.

SAM: I'm your buddy, Wayne. Talk to me. *[Pause]*

WAYNE: If there's anything to tell, she'll have to tell you herself.

SAM: One of those, eh.

WAYNE: One of what?

SAM: Nothing, nothing. I can certainly understand you being loyal to her and I respect that. How much longer you have in school?

WAYNE: A few months.

SAM: And I take it you're going on to university?

WAYNE: I plan to.

SAM: To study what?

WAYNE: Medicine.

SAM: Aaaha, medicine. Good. Very good. Scholarship?

WAYNE: I hope so.

SAM: Any way you cut it, it's going to call for a lot of money. Even with a scholarship you will still need a lot of money over a long period of time.

WAYNE: I know that.

SAM: And if you do get a scholarship they'll bond you. For the rest of your life if you not careful. And stupid politicians and flunky civil servants will treat you like they own you.

WAYNE: For a few years, maybe.

SAM: For at least the next fifteen years. A smart boy like you must be able to do better than that.

WAYNE: How?

SAM: Good question. I'll put my mind to it and come up with something. Think you might be interested?

WAYNE: Yes, sir. Very much so.

SAM: Good. I love to see smart grassroots kids get ahead. Kids with drive and determination. I always say education is the great equalizer, but the poor pay too dearly for it. Yes, I'll put my mind to it and come up with something good for you.

WAYNE: I appreciate that, sir.

SAM: Get you something else to drink?

WAYNE: No thank you, sir. I'm just going to work on the dance a bit more.

SAM: Without your partner?

WAYNE: She'll be here.

SAM: Well, make sure you knock 'em dead tonight.

WAYNE: We plan to do just that.

SAM: Catch you later.

*[He exits. Wayne turns on his cassette player and
is practicing his dance steps as Cynthia enters.
She turns down the music]*

CYNTHIA: Hi. Miss me?

WAYNE: Come ley me show you something here. Let's see
             if we can work it in.

CYNTHIA: No way. The dance stays as it is. Anything new at
             this late stage is only going to confuse me.

WAYNE: Dummy.

CYNTHIA: Dummy yourself.

WAYNE: So wha' you say happen to you all this week?

CYNTHIA: I ain't tell you? Guess not. Hardly saw you at all
             and you didn't even call me once.

WAYNE: I called. Left several messages at home and at
             work.

CYNTHIA: I would have called you back if you had a phone,
             but...*[Pause]* Roger called me.

WAYNE: In truth?!

CYNTHIA: Four or five times, this week alone, he calling me.

WAYNE: To say what?

CYNTHIA: Not a line, as you know Wayne, not one word, far
             more phone call, in two and a half years, and now,
             all of a sudden, he breaking me down wid calls,
             telling me I must pack up, resign my job and come
             join him.

WAYNE: And?

CYNTHIA: And? I tell him to go to hell! Two and a half years, you know, man. And he know the condition he left me in. But yet not a word, not an inquiry to see if am alive or dead or if I eat. In two and a half years! And now I must join him? No, man.

WAYNE: I agree with you, but what you mother saying?

CYNTHIA: He talk to her too, for long. She think I should go, but no way. Not me. That bastard! Anyway, let's talk about it some other time because it getting me upset. Come telling me 'bout he not taking no for an answer.

WAYNE: On another matter, Cyn. Wha' Mr. Drum…

CYNTHIA: Don't call me "Cyn!"

WAYNE: Okay, Cynthia. Wha' Mr. Drummonds give you?

CYNTHIA: What you talking 'bout?

WAYNE: When I came back with the drinks he was giving you something.

CYNTHIA: Oh God, yes. Boy, you fast, eh?

WAYNE: What was it?

CYNTHIA: None you damn business. What I did with it at all? *[She searches, finds envelope and opens it. It contains ten $20 bills]* See? 20, 40, 60, 80, 100. 20, 40, 60, 80, 200.

WAYNE: Two hundred dollars? For what?

CYNTHIA: For what? For me.

WAYNE: You goin' keep it?

CYNTHIA: De sun goin' rise tomorrow?

WAYNE: You can't keep it, Cyn.

CYNTHIA: You dotish or what? And don't call me "Cyn."

WAYNE: Cynthia! Christ, what's the matter with you?

CYNTHIA: My name is Cynthia. I don't like to be called Cyn, so don't call me Cyn.

WAYNE: All I'm saying is that I think you should give him back his money.

CYNTHIA: I didn't ask him for it, you know. I didn't beg him for no money. Is he take it on himself and give it to me.

WAYNE: All the more reason you should give it back to him.

CYNTHIA: I didn't see you giving him back the change he gave you earlier.

WAYNE: That's different altogether.

CYNTHIA: Different how? He offer you money and you keep it. He offer me money and I keeping it too. Where's the difference?

WAYNE: You know exactly where the difference is.

CYNTHIA: You know how long it take me to work for $200, boy?

WAYNE: Just give it back to him, Cynthia.

CYNTHIA: You know what I could do with this $200?

WAYNE: Regardless.

CYNTHIA: And what is $200 to a man like Sam Drummonds?

WAYNE: Why you think he give it to you?

CYNTHIA: Who the hell cares why?

WAYNE: Well, you should care.

CYNTHIA: Why the hell should I? He gee me his money, I
              keep it, I spent it, that's, it. Fini! Kaputs! Kapeesh?

WAYNE: It's not that simple.

CYNTHIA: Couldn't be simpler. You're young, Wayne. You
              don't understand these things.

WAYNE: I understand this perfectly well. And you only
              pretending not to understand.

CYNTHIA: I understand one thing: De man gee me 200
              bucks and ah keeping it. That's all.

WAYNE: When you keep his money all you're doing is
              saying yes to him.

CYNTHIA: Yes to him for what?

WAYNE: Think about it.

CYNTHIA: No. You tell me.

WAYNE: You agree to sell yourself.

CYNTHIA: Don't be a damn ass.

WAYNE: Just think about it and you'll see what I'm saying
              is true.

CYNTHIA: You really believe Sam Drummonds gee me this
              $200 just so he could jump me body?

WAYNE: Why else?

CYNTHIA: As if I'm some ole whore?

WAYNE: In a sort of way, yes.

CYNTHIA: I want to meet the man who could buy me for $200.

WAYNE: Why would he just up and give you $200?

CYNTHIA: Because he's a nice ole man. Because he can afford to be kind. Because he likes me and wants me to be happy. *[Pause]* You don't think that's possible? You don't believe there're people in the world like that?

WAYNE: Maybe, but I don't think that's what's happening here.

CYNTHIA: Why not?

WAYNE: Because of how he looks at you when he doesn't think I'm seeing. He strips you naked with his eyes.

CYNTHIA: *[In jest]* Dirty ole man.

WAYNE: That's why I'm asking you not to keep his money.

CYNTHIA: Well, Wayne, as long as it's only his eyes he's stripping me with, at $200 a strip, he can undress me as much as he likes. I'm keeping the money and I'm not even going to buy you one drink out of it.

WAYNE: Don't even talk to me until you give it back.

CYNTHIA: Don't hold your breath because I'm definitely, positively not giving it back.

WAYNE: Give him back his money, Cynthia.

CYNTHIA: I am not giving it back! Now will you just get the hell off my case and stop bugging me.

WAYNE: Sometimes you really make me sick. *[He exits]*

CYNTHIA: Be sick all you want, Wayne Cabey. You could puke your guts out all over Heaven for all I care.

             [Tony enters]

TONY: Oh yes?

CYNTHIA: I am not talking to you. Get lost.

TONY: Hey, I've been trying to get you alone all night and now I finally manage it, that's how you talk to me?

CYNTHIA: I'm not talking to you, man.

TONY: Hey! Come on.

CYNTHIA: You had no right to hurt Wayne like that.

TONY: Come on. He's a tough, strong boy.

CYNTHIA: No right! *[Pause]*

TONY: Okay, maybe I should not have hurt him, but it's all your fault.

CYNTHIA: My fault?

TONY: Hey, come here, let me tell you how. The mere thought of you in someone else's arms brings out the beast in me. That's all.

CYNTHIA: Oh, Darling. *[They embrace and kiss passion- ately. Tony tries to break off]* What's the matter?

TONY: Let's go out here. *[He leads her to the open field]*

CYNTHIA: *[Pulling away]* Not one damn.

TONY: We're not exactly private, you know.

CYNTHIA: When you going to stop being ashamed of me?

TONY: I'm not ashamed of you.

CYNTHIA: Oh yes you are.

TONY: Really, I'm not.

CYNTHIA: So, why you pulling away from me and pulling me
              out into some field like I'm cattle?

TONY: I don't want the whole world poking its nose into
              our business.

CYNTHIA: We're all alone, Tony.

TONY: Alone in a public place? You never could tell who
              would be coming out here in the next minute.

CYNTHIA: I'm sick and tired of this hiding and seeking, man.
              I'm just not a hide and seek woman, and I'm tired
              telling you that.

TONY: I'll make it up to you later, okay. We'll do all the
              hugging and kissing and whatever else then.
              Okay?

CYNTHIA: Same old story every time.

TONY: Believe me, honey, I'll make it up to you like you
              wouldn't believe. *[Pause]* So tell me now, what
              happened with you and Wayne?

CYNTHIA: What?

TONY: What were you and Wayne quarreling about?

CYNTHIA: We weren't quarreling.

TONY: So what was it then.

CYNTHIA: That's me and Wayne business.

TONY: I see. *[Pause]*

CYNTHIA: Angry?

TONY: No. I'm beside myself with joy.

CYNTHIA: My sweet baby is angry. *[She goes to embrace him]* Oh, I forgot I'm not supposed to touch him in public. We're barely allowed to talk to each other like two strangers.

TONY: I'm not amused, Cynthia. I'm not the least bit amused.

CYNTHIA: *[Touching her pocket where she had placed the $200]* Well, my learned friend, maybe you could amuse me by telling me what a girl should do if a strange man makes her a gift of $200.

TONY: Some man gave you $200?

CYNTHIA: No, no. Not me. A friend of mine.

TONY: Which friend?

CYNTHIA: I can't tell you that.

TONY: Why not?

CYNTHIA: She told me in confidence.

TONY: Who is it?

CYNTHIA: I don't want to tell you.

TONY: Well, I want to know, so tell me.

CYNTHIA: Look, just forget I mentioned it. Okay?

TONY: So, some strange man gave your...mysterious friend $200?

CYNTHIA: I said let's...

TONY: Is that what you're telling me?

CYNTHIA: That's right.

TONY: Out of the clear blue sky?

CYNTHIA: Well, not exactly out of the clear blue sky. He met
             her yesterday and gave her an envelope with a
             card. The card said, "I think of you often" and in
             it was $200.

TONY: That's it?

CYNTHIA: That's it.

TONY: Can't be more out of the clear blue sky than that.

CYNTHIA: So she asked me what I think she should do. I told
             her she should spend the damn money. What you
             think?

TONY: Well, it depends.

CYNTHIA: Answered like a true lawyer. Depends on what?

TONY: Whether or not the girl is willing to sell what the
             guy is looking to buy.

CYNTHIA: What's all this crap about buying and selling?

TONY: Manna doesn't exactly fall from Heaven any more,
             you know. A guy puts out that kind of bread, he's
             looking for goods and/or services in return.

CYNTHIA: What if the guy is her uncle or father?

TONY: Well, is he?

CYNTHIA: No, but maybe he just want to be nice to her. And
             even if he is looking for something in return,
             what's to stop her from spending his money and
             not delivering.

TONY: She could get away with that once, twice, maybe even three times. But if she wants to keep him putting out, she's going to have to start putting out too.

CYNTHIA: I don't agree.

TONY: It doesn't matter if you agree or not. It's a law of life, like gravity.

CYNTHIA: One shot. She takes his money and run and that's it. What could he do her?

TONY: Absolutely nothing.

CYNTHIA: As a matter of fact, if he keeps giving her money, as long as she doesn't ask him for it, she could take it, do what she wants with it and never give him a thing in return.

TONY: He's never going to keep giving indefinitely…unless he's getting something in return.

CYNTHIA: So he stops giving, she stops taking. No big deal.

TONY: Only that by now she's hooked. All that easy money. She needs to keep it flowing in.

CYNTHIA: Doesn't have to be. She takes his money till he comes to his senses and stops giving. And she doesn't give him one damn thing in return.

TONY: But chances are she will want a new outfit to wear to Heaven. And a new hair do. Maybe it's the end of the month, so she has bills to pay. She has to get some groceries. There are a hundred good reasons why she needs that money. And once she keeps taking it, sooner or later she too is going to have to put out. So, if she doesn't want to get trapped, the best thing is not to take his money in the first place.

CYNTHIA: That's the same foolish talk I was getting from Wayne.

TONY: You discussed this with Wayne?

CYNTHIA: Sure, I discussed it with him.

TONY: Is there anything you don't discuss with him?

CYNTHIA: Please, don't start that again.

TONY: I would really like to know the truth about what's going on between the two of you.

CYNTHIA: For the last and final time, Wayne is my friend. You don't expect me to have any friends?

TONY: The final result of any friendship between a man and a woman is sex.

CYNTHIA: Says who?

TONY: I'm telling you that. Let them deny it all they want. Let them avoid it all they want. Let them run away from it. Once the friendship continues, sooner or later, they're going to end up in bed.

CYNTHIA: Well, I don't believe that.

TONY: You don't have to believe the earth is round either.

CYNTHIA: Look, why don't we go dance or something?

TONY: What's the 'or something?'

CYNTHIA: You really want to hear?

TONY: Sure I want to hear. Tell me. *[Dilys enters]*

DILYS: There you go disappearing on me again. Come, let's dance. Your favorite song is playing.

CYNTHIA: He's talking to me. Can't you see?

DILYS: Excuse me, and who are you?

CYNTHIA: That's for me to know and for you to find out.

DILYS: Well, you can rest assured that I haven't the
              slightest interest in finding out. However, this
              man here happens to be my husband and if you
              don't mind I'd like to dance with him now. Come
              on, Tony, let's go.

TONY: *[To Cynthia]* Look, the best place for us to discuss
              that title deed is really my office. So, why don't you
              drop in and see me early next week?

CYNTHIA: Man!...Just go 'bout you business, eh.

DILYS: Title Deed?

TONY: You know how it is, darling. Even in the disco-
              theque people always want to talk business with
              me. *[They exit]*

CYNTHIA: Hell! *[Sam enters]*

SAM: What's my favorite dancer doing out here all by
              her pretty self? Tell you what, why don't we leave?
              You could come to my house, listen to records, sip
              as much wine or beer as you like, swim in my pool,
              sleep, and, tomorrow, I'll serve you breakfast in
              bed. How about it?

CYNTHIA: No thank you.

SAM: We can skip the breakfast in bed part if you have
              to leave before tomorrow. Or if you prefer, I can
              take you straight to your home.

CYNTHIA: I'm not ready to go home.

SAM: Then let's just go somewhere else.

CYNTHIA: I'm staying right here.

SAM: The night is not going to get any better for you
            here, you know.

CYNTHIA: What you mean?

SAM: You know what I mean.

CYNTHIA: No, I don't.

SAM: You happy with your little gift?

CYNTHIA: Your $200?

SAM: Your $200.

CYNTHIA: You want it back?

SAM: Of course not.

CYNTHIA: Nobody is going to buy me for $200.

SAM: You for $200? That couldn't even pay for the dirt
            under your fingernails. Look, Cynthia, let me
            explain what's happening here. When I spotted
            you along the road earlier this evening, looking a
            ride into town, I couldn't believe my good fortune.
            And let me say here, if you were my woman, you
            would never have to stand by the side of any road
            looking for any ride to any place. I would treat you
            like a queen, as you ought to be treated.

CYNTHIA: You don't even know me.

SAM: True. In fact, before tonight I could only remember
            seeing you two or three times. But each time I got
            this feeling I should get to know you better. So,
            when you came into the car, I was determined to
            talk to you, but you wouldn't let me make any
            head way, so I said forget it. Only I couldn't forget
            it. After I dropped you off, I couldn't get you off my
            mind. I went home and went to bed but you were
            still right there in the room with me. I tried closing

by eyes but your face was painted onto my eye lids. So I got dressed and came back here to look for you. Now, I am not a man of many fancy words and I don't like beating around the bush, so let me put my cards straight on the table. I want to take you home tonight. And I want you to give us a chance to get to know each other better. And then, I want you to give me the chance, the opportunity, the privilege to take care of you in the grand style you deserve.

CYNTHIA: Well, suppose you were a man of many fancy words? You'd talk life right back into the dead.

SAM: Is that supposed to be a compliment?

CYNTHIA: I'm not sure. You sound too much like a damn politician.

SAM: Ah, but there is a difference. For the most part they're just full of ole talk. When you get to know me better you'll find out that I have both the capability and the capacity to deliver what I promise.

CYNTHIA: IF I get to know you better, you mean.

SAM: No, my dear, WHEN.

CYNTHIA: Don't be so flipping cock-sure with me, buster.

            [Tony enters]

TONY: Am I interrupting something?

SAM: Not at all.

TONY: Let me talk to you a minute, Sam.

SAM: *[Moving towards Tony]* Shoot.

TONY: Do me a favor would you?

SAM: If I can, sure.

TONY: Go dance with Dilys and keep her busy for me for a bit. Okay?

SAM: Sure. No problem at all. *[Exits]*

TONY: What was that old fart saying to you?

CYNTHIA: You have a hell of a nerve.

TONY: I'm not joking, Cynthia.

CYNTHIA: Get lost.

TONY: What did Sam Drummonds say to you?

CYNTHIA: What did your wife say to you?

TONY: Look, leave Dilys out of this.

CYNTHIA: What did your frigging wife say to you, Tony Thompson, what did she say to you? Until you can answer me that don't come asking me no shit. *[He makes to slap her]* Hit me! Yes go ahead and hit me, if is trouble you looking for.

TONY *[Bringing his hand to rest on her cheek without slapping her, he fondles it roughly]* A fine cheek. A lovely, delicate jaw. Try never to give me cause to break it.

CYNTHIA: Tonight was supposed to be my night. Our night together. We planned it, Tony.

TONY: I know, but would you please try to be under-standing?

CYNTHIA: I'm tired of trying to be understanding.

TONY: I completely forgot today was my anniversary. I couldn't very well say to Dilys I wasn't taking her out tonight.

CYNTHIA: How charming. Well, what about Cynthia? What about giving Cynthia a little understanding for a change?

TONY: Oh, come on...

CYNTHIA: Don't 'oh-come-on' me. You should have let me know our date was off so I didn't have to come down here like this for you and your wife to make an ass out of me.

TONY: Listen, I will take Dilys home early and come back for you so we can still spend some time together tonight.

CYNTHIA: Don't bother.

TONY: What you mean don't bother?

CYNTHIA: Just that. Someone else is already taking me home. So you can go home and stay home with your fat wife.

TONY: Quit fooling around, Cynthia.

CYNTHIA: You think I'm fooling around eh! Well I'll have you to know I'm dead serious.

TONY: You better not be.

CYNTHIA: Watch and see.

TONY: Who's taking you home?

CYNTHIA: None of your damn business, buster.

TONY: Why do I waste my breath asking? I'm the only person taking you home tonight.

CYNTHIA: Don't be so sure. I'm tired of this second string you're making me play. I want to go home first class tonight. And you know what my admirer said? He said If I was his woman I wouldn't have to stand by the road side begging any ride again—ever. He said he might even buy me my own car.

TONY: Sam Drummonds! That has to be Sam Drummonds, right?

CYNTHIA: And so what if it is?

TONY: And did he also invite you to his house to listen to music and sip wine, spend the night and have breakfast in bed?

CYNTHIA: How you know that?

TONY: It's his standard pitch, for god's sake. Only a sucker could fall for that bucket of crap.

CYNTHIA: He also invited me to swim in his pool.

TONY: Oh yes, I forgot that. Swim in his pool. *[He laughs]* Swim in his pool.

CYNTHIA: But does he have a pool?

TONY: Sure he does.

CYNTHIA: And does he have a stereo that plays music? And is his wine good. And is he able to put a woman up over night and give her breakfast in bed the next morning?

TONY: All of that is beside the point.

CYNTHIA: All of that is the point. If it exists, if it is real, if it is possible, if he can do what he says, how can it be crap? And considering my situation, what do I have to lose by accepting his invitation?

TONY: Cynthia, I want you to listen to me very carefully.
            And I want you to note that I'm not smiling, I'm not
            laughing and I'm definitely not joking. Under no
            circumstances are you to let Sam Drummonds
            take you home tonight.

CYNTHIA: Ha, ha, ha!

TONY: I don't want him taking you home. I don't want
            him anywhere near you.

CYNTHIA: Come to think of it he's not a bad looking guy. A
            little old maybe, but not at all bad.

TONY: Sam is not a man to fool with.

CYNTHIA: I'm sure.

TONY: I'm not joking, Cynthia, I don't want you messing
            with him.

CYNTHIA: I'm sick and tired of you messing with me, Tony
            Thompson. Messing up my whole life. You can't
            understand that?

TONY: You think I'm messing up your life? You want to
            see what it's like for your life to be messed up, get
            involved with Sam.

CYNTHIA: I'm not even listening to you. *[She crosses towards
            open field]*

TONY: Try and remember Roger McPherson.

CYNTHIA: I don't have to try.

TONY: Think about him all the time, eh?

CYNTHIA: What the hell you expect?

TONY: You know what his relationship was with Sam?

CYNTHIA: He didn't even know Sam.

TONY: So you think.

CYNTHIA: What was his relationship with Sam? *[Crosses back to Tony]*

TONY: I'm not sure you want to know.

CYNTHIA: Well, I'm sure I want to know, so tell me.

TONY: Under one condition.

CYNTHIA: And that is?

TONY: That you don't let Sam take you home.

CYNTHIA: Well, if you feel so strong about it, what can I say? I suppose you'll make arrangements for a taxi to take me home.

TONY: I'm taking you home. I told you that already.

CYNTHIA: Yes, of course, I forgot. So what was between Roger and Sam?

TONY: You know what business Sam is in?

CYNTHIA: He has some kind of gift shop, I think.

TONY: And what kind of shop is going to give him the kind of life-style he has? *[Pause]* His real business is drugs.

CYNTHIA: He...he...was in it with Roger?

TONY: He cultivated Roger because Roger was a pharmacist and could legally help him with his illegal business. It was he who got Roger involved in the first place and Roger to serve him well for many months. But when the Drug Enforcement Administration in the States tipped off the police here,

	Sam was also tipped off. So he arranged to walk away from it completely and let Roger take the heat.
CYNTHIA:	So that's who it was. Sam Drummonds. Sam Drummonds is that awful sonofabitch.
TONY:	And he's always on the look out for new talent. Anybody he can use. Which is why I don't want you getting close to him.
CYNTHIA:	Look how he hurt Roger, man. Look how he hurt me. You can't imagine how many times I said in my heart if I only find out who the bastard is I would kill him.
TONY:	It was also he who gave you that $200, right?
CYNTHIA:	What $200?
TONY:	The one you told me about earlier.
CYNTHIA:	I told you somebody gave me $200?
TONY:	Well…
CYNTHIA:	Well? Well? Don't try pulling any fast ones like that, Tony, because it's not going to work. I told you the money was given to a friend of mine. Why you can't believe me and let it rest?
TONY:	You know the answer to that already.
CYNTHIA:	Yes, I know.
TOGETHER:	Us lawyers don't make good believers.
TONY:	And you know why?
CYNTHIA:	I have a reasonably good idea.
TONY:	Because we see, every single day, what a truly shitful world this is.

CYNTHIA: I love you Tony, I really do, but sometimes this relationship makes me more miserable than I ever want to be.

TONY: It will get better, believe me. *[Wayne enters]*

WAYNE: It's time to get ready for the contest.

CYNTHIA: I almost forgot about that. I hope I haven't forgotten the steps. Check you later, Tony, got to get dressed. *[She kisses him on the cheeks and exists]*

TONY: Wayne, hold on a minute.

WAYNE: What?

TONY: Caught you off guard earlier with that hold , eh?

WAYNE: Man, just leave me alone, okay.

TONY: Come on, it's a useful grip for any tae-kwon-do man to learn. I'll show it to you.

WAYNE: No thanks.

TONY: I'm not going to hurt you, man. How's the shoulder now?

WAYNE: I'm in a hurry.

TONY: Look here, give it to me a minute. Relax. *[He massages Wayne's shoulder]* Okay, move it up and down, backwards and forwards. Move the whole arm around now. Up, two, three, four. And back, two, three, four. How's that?

WAYNE: Same as before.

TONY: Well, let's hope it doesn't kill you. *[Wayne starts to leave]* And by the way, Wayne, I admire the position you took regarding the $200.

WAYNE: What $200?

TONY: You know.

WAYNE: I don't know.

TONY: Sure you do.

WAYNE: I don't know what you're talking about.

TONY: The $200 Mr. Drummonds gave to Cynthia.

WAYNE: Oh.

TONY: I agree with you one hundred percent. She ought to give it back.

WAYNE: I told you, I don't know what you're talking about.

TONY: She told me all about it. What you said to her makes a lot of good sense.

WAYNE: I still don't know what you're talking about.

TONY: That's how you plan to play the game?

WAYNE: What game?

TONY: My mistake. Forget I mentioned it *[He turns away and Wayne again moves towards the exit]*

WAYNE: Tony.

TONY: Yeah?

WAYNE: Piss off!. *[He exits. Sam and Dilys enter]*

DILYS: What's the big attraction out here?

TONY: What you talking about?

DILYS: You're spending more time out here than dancing in the disco.

TONY: I don't like it when it's over-crowded.

DILYS: You're not going to watch the contest?

TONY: No. I don't think so.

DILYS: What about you, Sam?

SAM: I'm going to keep Tony company.

DILYS: Look at the two of you. Two spoil sports. I came out
             to enjoy myself and that's exactly what I'm going
             to do. See you guys later. *[She exits]*

SAM: Everything under control?

TONY: No tears.

SAM: As yet.

TONY: What's that supposed to mean?

SAM: Just a joke, my friend, just a joke.

TONY: Oh.

SAM: This is Heaven. There's not suppose to be any
             tears here - ever. *[Pause]* Wouldn't it be wonderful
             to live in a world without tears? Or even to have
             the assurance that after death we'd go to a place
             where there're no tears?

TONY: What the hell are you talking about?

SAM: Ahhhhh! Just that it's curious about Heaven,
             when you think about it.

TONY: If you think about it.

SAM: When you think about it. And at my age you get
             to thinking about it more and more.

TONY: How old are you, Sam?

SAM: A lot older than you, my friend. Old enough to
               start seriously pondering these things. Death,
               Heaven, Hell. Redemption, salvation. How did
               jealousy get into Heaven? Ever think of that? How
               did it manage to find its way into Lucifer's heart?
               And he went with one third of the angels, you
               know, Tony. A whopping 33.3%.

TONY: In an election you'd consider that a good showing,
               eh?

SAM: Exactly, precisely. Good enough to encourage
               anybody to try again. Which brings me to the
               heart of the matter. When all is said and done,
               when Christ comes again and sets up his king-
               dom, what guarantees do we have that in that
               New Jerusalem, that perfect Heaven, Lucifer will
               not find a way to try again?

TONY: Look, what we getting into all this heavy crap for?

SAM: Answer the question.

TONY: Well, according to my Bible, Lucifer will be bound
               hand and foot and cast into an everlasting lake of
               fire.

SAM: Ah! But who's to say that some new Lucifer, or
               Tony or Sam, will not look across his avenue of
               gold to his brother's house and think: he got a
               nicer mansion than me. His view is better. Pretty
               soon this ungrateful malcontent begins to agitate,
               begins to stir up trouble. And this time around he
               might be more effective than the first Lucifer. He
               might be able to swing 55 or 60%. What then?
               What would that make of all our pain and anguish
               and sacrifices?

TONY: You had too much to drink, Sam. That's the liquor
               talking. You should go home and sleep.

SAM: I'm at least as sober as you. If not more so.

TONY: Well, I never joke about things like Heaven. That's God's domain and I don't skylark with God. What I do know is that on earth you must be eternally on guard against treachery.

SAM: Yes?

TONY: TREACHERY! *[Slamming his hand on table]* How the hell you could be taking up $200 and giving it to my woman to come to your house for wine and music and breakfast?

SAM: How was I to know she's your woman?

TONY: Everybody knows she's my woman.

SAM: Including Dilys?

TONY: Dilys is not concerned with this.

SAM: Oh, really?

TONY: Of course, if you want to waste your money, don't let me stop you.

SAM: Seriously, I didn't know she was your woman. I thought your only woman was Dilys.

TONY: Oh, come on.

SAM: Seriously, I thought your only woman was your wife and the others are just...well...pussy.

TONY: I never think of a woman as being 'just pussy'.

SAM: Of course.

TONY: I'm serious.

SAM: Sure you are.

TONY: You think I'm joking but I'm very serious. I have more respect for women than that.

SAM: Naturally, Tony. I'm ashamed of myself for thinking otherwise. *[He laughs]*

TONY: You think it's funny, eh?

SAM: It's the most serious thing I've heard all night.

TONY: Well, there's something not so funny I've been meaning to talk to you about for some time.

SAM: Talk.

TONY: You're far too careless with your money, too conspicuous. You're drawing attention to yourself and that's not smart.

SAM: Is that a fact?

TONY: A fact, or a joke. It's up to you.

SAM: It wouldn't be a threat by any chance?

TONY: Just good advise from your lawyer. But you may laugh at it if you like.

SAM: When my lawyer offers free advise, that <u>is</u> serious. Or do you plan to invoice me later?

TONY: I'm really not joking, Sam. You have a good cover for your…operation, but think of it. Who's going to believe your gift and music shop can generate the kind of dollars needed to support your life-style? Of course it doesn't matter too much here because nobody really gives a damn one way or another about anything, but America has declared a world war on drugs and they have people sniffing around everywhere. It wouldn't hurt to be more cautious.

SAM: You're right, but don't forget your own operation.

TONY: I'm a lawyer.

SAM: Of course, and that has to be the perfect cover.

TONY: I also happen to be 100% legitimate.

SAM: Perhaps. But some of those characters I see you doing business with, are some of my best clients.

TONY: What does that have to do with me?

SAM: Think. How legitimate can they be? You don't have to be any genius to know that this 'off-shore' business you and them are wrapped up in is mostly scam.

TONY: I'm not involved in any scam. I provide a legal service and collect my fees, that's all.

SAM: You're missing the point.

TONY: You don't have a point.

SAM: The point is, our world is not perfect and we both profit from this simple fact.

TONY: What the hell you saying? You comparing my legitimate legal practice as a barrister and a solicitor with your gaddam drug peddling operation?

SAM: It feeds me and it feeds you.

TONY: It most assuredly does not feed me!

SAM: You may not wish to think so...

TONY: It doesn't frigging feed me, man!

SAM: Okay, okay. Whatever you say. But you should keep this in mind: if today, by any set of circumstances, the FBI, let's say, starts to poke its nose into my business, get ready for them poking their nose into yours by tomorrow.

TONY: You threatening me?

SAM: Damn right I'm threatening you!

TONY: Well, let them come. Let them come and start to poke. Better yet, let's bring them. Let's call the police now. Let's call the FBI, the DEA, the CIA and all if you like. Let's invite them to come take a look at our affairs.

SAM: Tony, Tony, my buddy, let's not be rash. Let's not lose our grip on things because of some silly twit of a girl…

TONY: I don't regard her as a silly twit.

SAM: Whatever.

TONY: She's my woman. And to be frank with you, I don't like people messing with my woman.

SAM: You will risk everything for this woman?

TONY: You're the one with something to risk, Sam, not me. *[A burst of excitement comes through from inside]*

SAM: Seems to me this wonderful woman of yours is inside having a ball with another man.

TONY: Wayne? Wayne is just a young punk.

SAM: And me?

TONY: You know what you are, you know who you are.

SAM:	Maybe you're taking Wayne too lightly. Maybe he'll dance away with first prize and with your woman as his bonus prize. What then?
TONY:	I already said all I have to say. *[More excitement from inside]*
SAM:	Sounds like they're having a wild time in there. *[Pause]* Sure you don't want to go check it out, make sure everything is…copacetic?
TONY:	Quite sure.
SAM:	Well, my buddy, look at it this way: you're in great company.
TONY:	What company?
SAM:	God is also jealous. *[He laughs. Cynthia and Wayne enter. She is in very high spirits, singing and dancing]*
CYNTHIA:	Oh my goodness gracious, weren't we smashing? Weren't we fantastic? Weren't we just out of this world?
TONY:	You're always fantastic.
CYNTHIA:	Well, weren't we? Now wait a minute, you didn't see our performance did you? You good for nothing so and so. How could you? Well, you missed the show of your life.
SAM:	How about a repeat performance?
CYNTHIA:	Not on your life.
SAM:	Come on, show us your stuff.
CYNTHIA:	No way.
TONY:	That's a great idea.

CYNTHIA: Forget it. You should have gotten up off your ass
            and come see us knock everybody dead. Too late
            now.

SAM: Did you win?

CYNTHIA: Don't ask me any question, you bastard!

SAM: Hey...?

TONY: Cynthia. Please.

CYNTHIA: I don't want him saying anything to me. Ask him
            to have nothing to do with me.

SAM: Now, wait a minute...

CYNTHIA: I'm serious, Tony. Ask this scum-bag to keep as
            far away from me as possible. Come on Wayne,
            let's go change. *[She starts to exit and comes face
            to face with Dilys who is on her way to the
            bathroom. They exchange looks and Dilys exits]*
            On second thought, let's do our dance out here.

WAYNE: What?

CYNTHIA: You heard. Let's show our stuff.

WAYNE: You're crazy.

CYNTHIA: I'm serious.

WAYNE: You can't be. Forget it.

CYNTHIA: Let's do it, Wayne.

WAYNE: I'm not going to dance for those two guys.

CYNTHIA: Then dance for me. I danced for you inside. Now
            I'm asking you to dance for me out here.

WAYNE: Really, Cynthia...

CYNTHIA: Come on. *[She drags him to the dance area]* Start the music. *[He does and they dance with great confidence and passion. Dilys comes out of bathroom and stands upstage watching. When the dance ends both men clap wildly]*

DILYS: Really now, who is that girl?

CYNTHIA: Thank you so much folks. We're glad you loved us. If you want you may leave a token of your appreciation in the hat at the door. But right now our fans are waiting so we must be off. Let's go, partner. *[She drags Wayne with her and says directly to Dilys]:* Don't call us. We'll call you.

[Cynthia and Wayne exit]

BLACK OUT

ACT TWO

Same as Act One. No time has elapsed. The action continues from exactly where it stopped at the end of Act One.

DILYS: Gentlemen, I asked you a question. Who was that girl?

TONY: Her name is Cynthia Corbette. Now, if you don't mind, let's all go inside and have some more champagne.

DILYS: Who is she?

TONY: I just told you.

DILYS: What does she do?

TONY: She's a civil servant, I think.

DILYS: You think. And one of your clients?

TONY: Yes. She's one of my clients.

DILYS: How come she was dancing for you?

SAM: I asked her to, Dilys. That was my doing.

DILYS: And of course she was only too happy to oblige. I wonder why?

SAM: She loves to dance.

DILYS: Sam, let Tony answer me.

TONY: Hey, why the cross-examination? *[Pause]*

DILYS: Just that she's so...pretty. You don't find her pretty?

TONY: She's okay.

DILYS: That's all? Just okay?

TONY: Sure she's pretty, but so are you.

DILYS: Not like her.

TONY: In my eyes you're the prettiest woman in the whole wide world.

DILYS: Maybe I'm getting a little too old for you.

TONY: You're my queen and my angel. Don't ever loose sight of that. My queen and my angel. Always.

DILYS: So pretty. And so young. So...fresh.

TONY: Forget about her, sweetheart. Believe me, she's nothing to me. Absolutely nothing. So put her out of your mind and let's enjoy ourselves.

DILYS: A client.

TONY: A client! That's all.

DILYS: Well, I don't believe you.

TONY: What!

DILYS: I said I don't believe you.

TONY: You don't believe me?

DILYS: Yes. I don't believe you one little bit!

TONY: You gone crazy?

DILYS: Something is going on between you and that girl
          and I want to know what it is.

TONY: You definitely gone off your mind. You gone clean
          off you fu...cotton-picking mind!

SAM: Hey, Tony...

TONY: Stay out of this, Sam. Look, woman, who the hell
          you think you talking to like that? How dare you
          even think...

SAM: Tony! What you getting steamed up about? Relax,
          man. Don't spoil her night. Let it pass. *[Pause]*

TONY: Look, if you lost your senses, try and find them
          quick. When you do, I'm inside. *[He storms out]*

DILYS: He has such a nasty temper. Thanks.

SAM: No need to thank me.

DILYS: You must forgive me, cous. I'm not usually like
          this.

SAM: Maybe you need to stand up to him more often.

DILYS: Must be the drink. Maybe I've had too much to
          drink.

SAM: Really, you should consider standing up to him a
          bit more.

DILYS: This jealous wife bit is not becoming. Not becom-
          ing at all. And definitely not me.

SAM: You heard what I said?

DILYS: You saw how he got on just now?

SAM: Stop allowing him to intimidate you.

DILYS: How come you're telling me this? How come you're
            not taking up for him as usual?

SAM: I don't like what I just saw.

DILYS: You've seen it before, and it never bothered you
            before, so why is it bothering you now?

SAM: You're perfectly right, if it doesn't bother you, why
            should I let it bother me?

DILYS: I stand up to him, you know, Sam, but in matters
            of importance. Just now I went too far over
            stupidness.

SAM: Whatever makes you happy.

DILYS: I'll go look for him.

SAM: He expects you to come running after him. Don't.
            Leave him alone. Let him come to his senses and
            he'll be running back to look for you soon enough.
            [Wayne enters] Any word from the judges?

WAYNE: Not yet. *[Pointing out the cassette player]* I forgot
            this.

SAM: I've been keeping an eye on it for you.

WAYNE: Thanks.

DILYS: I really must go look for him, Sam. Excuse me.
            [She exits]

SAM: Where's your dance partner?

WAYNE: With your friend Tony, if you must know.

SAM: You don't like that, do you?

WAYNE: Do you?

SAM: Maybe his wife will catch him redhanded.

WAYNE: What good will that do?

SAM: You might be surprised. She may take him home
            and keep him home. Leave the course clear...for
            you.

WAYNE: Wouldn't make any difference to me.

SAM: A most attractive girl, this Cynthia. Hell, a stun-
            ning girl. But you musn't let her steal you heart.
            Eh, ole buddy?

WAYNE: Why you say that?

SAM: Because, more than likely, she would break it.
            Probably caused you untold pain already, right?
            Right, ole buddy?

WAYNE: Well...

SAM: You have to protect yourself from women like her,
            Wayne. 'Cause if you not careful, she will cause
            you even more pain. And pain, woman pain, can
            wreck even the strongest man.

WAYNE: She and I are just good friends, okay?

SAM: Just good friends?

WAYNE: That's right.

SAM: Good. I'm happy to hear that.

WAYNE: Why?

SAM: One of the most profitable lessons a young man
                can learn is how to handle women. And you know
                what the key to handling them is? Understanding
                them. And the only way you could understand
                them is not to get emotionally tied up with them.
                You understand?

WAYNE: Yes, sir.

SAM: You think you understand Cynthia?

WAYNE: Sometimes. But really, sir, I prefer not to discuss
                her.

SAM: You think you know her well?

WAYNE: As well as can be expected.

SAM: What would you say if I told you I'm going to take
                her home with me tonight?

WAYNE: You?

SAM: That's right.

WAYNE: To your house?

SAM: All the way home to my house.

WAYNE: No way. No possible way!

SAM: Look and learn.

WAYNE: There's no way on earth Cynthia will do that.

SAM: I'm glad you think so.

WAYNE: I know her, Mr. Drummonds, and I'm telling you
                she won't.

SAM: You have a lot to learn, Wayne. And you know
                something, the truly important lessons about life
                and women not in any text book. You either born

with the ability to grasp them or you destined forever to be a sort of idiot, matters not how much school you go to. The question is, do you have this ability or not?

WAYNE: I hope so.

SAM: Because, if you do, I'd send you to university myself.

WAYNE: You would?

SAM: Sure I would. I've thought about it since we spoke earlier and I sure would. And let me tell you, you wouldn't have to scrunt. Living in some roach-invested dingy room, washing dishes in some stinking restaurant to help make ends meet while you should be studying your lessons. Noosireee! I'll take good care of you and all of your financial needs. I'll guide you. And somewhere along the line, I hope we'll become...well...business part-ners. If that happens, I'll make you more money than if you could print it yourself.

WAYNE: Why would you do this for me?

SAM: Well, in the first place, I can afford to do it. In the second place, setting up a special scholarship fund, without strings, for bright poor-people chil-dren is something I've been thinking of doing for sometime. You could be the first to benefit from it, if, of course, you are deserving. But this is not the place to talk about it. Come see me at my home anytime tomorrow afternoon, let's begin to dis-cuss your...well...glorious future. Okay? Okay ole buddy?

WAYNE: I'll be there.

            [Dilys returns]

SAM: Couldn't find him?

DILYS: I found him.

SAM: You spoke to him?

DILYS: No. *[She sits by herself]*

WAYNE: You'll be out here for a while, sir?

SAM: I'll be here.

WAYNE: *[Indicating cassette player]* Could you continue to keep an eye on this for me please?

SAM: No problem.

WAYNE: Later.

                [Wayne Exits]

SAM: So what's the trouble?

DILYS: He's busy. Busy talking to that girl. They were talking intensely, as if quarrelling or something.

SAM: Yes.

DILYS: At one point she produced a handful of money and pushed it at him, but he refused it.

SAM: Money, eh?

DILYS: You think he's giving her money?

SAM: He saw you?

DILYS: I don't think so.

SAM: And you said nothing to him?

DILYS: Nothing.

                [Tony enters]

TONY: I'm ready to go.

DILYS: Already? It's not even two yet.

TONY: Come on.

DILYS: I was hoping we could dance some more. One more?

TONY: It's too crowded. I don't like it when it's so crowded. We're going home.

DILYS: Whatever you say. You want us to go, we go.

TONY: I'll get the car. Meet me up front in a minute. See you around, Sam.

SAM: You bet. Take care, buddy. *[Tony Exits]* So I guess this is where you get tucked into bed and sent off to never, never land.

DILYS: What are you talking about?

SAM: Never mind.

DILYS: No, Sam. Tell me.

SAM: Forget it. *[Pause]*

DILYS: Sam, what's the truth about the dancer girl?

SAM: You're back on that again.

DILYS: Just asking.

SAM: Why you ask?

DILYS: Call it female intuition. I just sense there's something there I should know.

SAM: There's nothing there you should know.

DILYS: I know there is, and I want to find out what it is.

SAM: If I were you, I'd leave it alone.

DILYS: I don't want to leave it alone.

SAM: Do yourself a favor, Dilys, let it rest.

DILYS: I can't let it rest till I get to the bottom of it. So be
              a darling and tell me who she is.

SAM: I don't want you to get hurt.

DILYS: Aha! So there is something going on to hurt me?

SAM: I didn't say that.

DILYS: Tony is in something with that girl. I know it. I just
              know it.

SAM: Go home, go to bed, have a good rest. Tomorrow
              you'll wake up and not even remember she exists.

DILYS: You may as well tell me what's gong on, Sam,
              because I'll never stop digging until I find out the
              truth.

SAM: Truth can be painful.

DILYS: I want to know the truth.

SAM: Well, I'm not going to be the one to tell you.

DILYS: Sam, if the fact that we are family means anything
              to you, if you care about me even one little bit, you
              would tell me.

SAM: Tell you what. After you get home tonight, Tony is
              going to find some reason to leave the house.
              When he does give him a head-start, then jump in
              your car and come back here.

DILYS: For what ? Why should he leave home? And why
              should I come back here?

SAM: Just do as I tell you. Let him leave, then come right back here.

DILYS: He's coming back here?

SAM: Come and see.

DILYS: For the girl?

SAM: Just do what I tell you and ask no more questions.

DILYS: Naah. No! I couldn't do that. I can't spy on Tony .

SAM: Good. So be it. *[Pause]*

DILYS: You know, we've been married for ten years and I couldn't tell you for sure if he ever had another woman?

SAM: Really?

DILYS: I've had my suspicions, yes. People have told me things, of course. But I don't know for a fact because I have never put out myself to know and he has never flaunted any of them in my face.

SAM: And, as the saying goes, wha' eye no see heart no grieve.

DILYS: I guess.

SAM: Great. So we're right back where we started. For your own sake, take my advise and forget the whole matter. Go home with your husband, stop asking questions and continue to live in peace.

DILYS: Besides, I don't think this girl is his type anyway.

SAM: You're still dwelling on it?

DILYS: You're right. I shouldn't dwell on it. I really should just forget the whole thing. *[Silence]* Well, I musn't keep Tony waiting. Good night, Sam. Take care of your self.

SAM: Innocence! How I admire it, adore it, love it. But it's a virtue not suited to this life.

DILYS: Trying to tell me something, Sam?

SAM: I'm just hoping that whatever happens tonight, you will stand firm. When Tony comes up with his excuse to leave you at home alone in your nice cozy bed, promise me that whatever it takes, you will just bury your head in your pillow and go to sleep.

DILYS: I don't even think it will get to that. I have such a celebration planned for him he'll need to sleep for a week when it's over.

SAM: That's my Dilys. *[Tony enters]*

TONY: All set?

DILYS: All set.

TONY: I thought you changed your mind. Come, let's get out of here *[He leaves]*

DILYS: Bye, Sam.

SAM: I'll see you soon.

DILYS: No you won't.

SAM: Good.

DILYS: You must come to Heaven more often, it's good for you. Night, night.

[She exits. Sam does a gleeful little jig, turns on the cassette player and dances. Cynthia enters. He dances towards her with his arms outstretched]

SAM: You have got to be the most fabulously sexy dancer on earth.

CYNTHIA: And you have got to be the biggest fink, the greatest crap artist and the vilest serpent on earth. Have nothing else to say to me again—ever! You hear me?

SAM: My, my, my.

CYNTHIA: And as for your $200 you can take it and stuff it for all I care. *[She flings the money at him]*

SAM: You're going to explain what this is all about?

CYNTHIA: I don't have to explain nothing to you, man. Just piss off and leave me alone. *[She starts to exit]*

SAM: Cynthia! Cynthia! Wait!

CYNTHIA: Wait for what?

SAM: I want to talk to you.

CYNTHIA: You can't understand English? I don't want to talk to you, ever again!

SAM: So you sentence and condemn me for nothing, without giving me a chance to defend myself.

CYNTHIA: For nothing? For nothing you say?

SAM: Yes! For nothing. *[He picks up money]*

CYNTHIA: Roger McPherson! Think about Roger McPherson and tell me if that's for nothing.

SAM: What does Roger have to do with any of this?

CYNTHIA: I'm glad you asked. You filth, you snake, you…

SAM: Will you stop calling me names and tell me what
             I'm supposed to have done?

CYNTHIA: You know what you did, man. You damn well
             know what you did.

SAM: I don't have a clue what you're talking about.

CYNTHIA: You screwed Roger good and plenty, that's what
             you did.

SAM: Screwed him? I was the boy's best friend.

CYNTHIA: You made friends with him because you knew he
             was a pharmacist and wanted to use him.

SAM: I'm listening.

CYNTHIA: Then you got him to order all of those drugs for
             you. And you gave him the stamp from the
             hospital so the order would look official.

SAM: Who told you that?

CYNTHIA: Never mind who told me! Then when they caught
             up with him, you promised him if he kept his
             mouth shut you would make him rich for life and
             arrange for him to go and live in America. Then
             you let them send him to jail and deport him back
             to Guyana without one cent.

SAM: Lies! All Lies.

CYNTHIA: It's true. And you damn well know it's true. Did
             you stop to consider his girlfriend?

SAM: I didn't even know he had a girlfriend.

CYNTHIA: His girlfriend who was pregnant? Who got kicked
             out of school to bring her child into the world
             without a father.

SAM: I had no idea about any girlfriend or any child.

CYNTHIA: Well, I am that girl. And I'm damn angry about what you did to him, and to me, and to my son.

SAM: Well, I can understand that. I understand that entirely.

CYNTHIA: You can't begin to understand it. You can't begin to understand what it is to be shunned, scorned and ridiculed by all your friends at 15. *[Pause]* All except Wayne. *[Pause]* And you can't begin to understand the burden of bringing up a child all by yourself. That is what you put me through.

SAM: I wasn't born with any silver spoon in my mouth, Cynthia. I know from bitter first hand experience how tough life is. So believe me, I understand. But the truth is, you accusing me of doing things I never did.

CYNTHIA: Don't give me that, man. Roger told me all about it himself. The only thing he wouldn't tell me was who set him up, for fear of what they would do him, or worse yet do me and the child. But I found out tonight who did it. You, Samuel Drummonds! You and nobody else but you, so don't come telling me no nonsense.

SAM: Okay, let's back up a bit. Why you giving me back the money?

CYNTHIA: I don't need you or your blood money, man. Just leave me alone and go to hell.

SAM: Surely the smart thing to do is pocket the money and still tell me go to hell.

CYNTHIA: The smart thing for you to do.

SAM: For anybody to do. And you seem like a smart girl
              to me. So giving me back the money doesn't make
              sense.

CYNTHIA: My boyfriend does not want me to keep your
              money. And I do not want to keep your filthy
              money either.

SAM: Aha! Now I get it. But you're really not so smart
              after all. I give you something, that's between me
              and you. You had no call running to your boy-
              friend blabbing off your mouth about it.

CYNTHIA: Me, blabbing off my mouth? Don't make me
              laugh! You're the one who ran to tell him, bragging
              off about what and what not you're going to do
              with me for a lousy 200 bucks. As if 200 bucks is
              money.

SAM: Where's your senses? You think I'd say such a
              thing to your boyfriend?

CYNTHIA: You didn't know he's my boyfriend.

SAM: Who doesn't know he's your boyfriend?

CYNTHIA: You didn't! You hardly knew I even existed until
              tonight.

SAM: Tony is my lawyer and my personal friend. I have
              to know who his girlfriend is.

CYNTHIA: If he's such a good friend, then why you trying to
              pick me up in the first place?

              [Wayne Enters]

WAYNE: Hey, Cynthia, standing by?

CYNTHIA: For what?

WAYNE: For when they call the winners, dumb, dumb.

CYNTHIA: Oh, yes, of course.

WAYNE: You'll be here?

CYNTHIA: Yes, I'll be here.

WAYNE: Cool. I'll come and get you.

CYNTHIA: Hey, Wayne, you want to hear something? Is this son-of-a-bitch you see here made them deport Roger, you know.

WAYNE: Mr. Drummonds?

CYNTHIA: What the hell Mr. Drummonds? This scumbag here that you look up to and respect is worse than a snake. Nobody dealing more drugs than him, you know.

WAYNE: No, man, Cyn. Not Mr. Drummonds.

CYNTHIA: Think, Wayne. How else could he get all this money he throwing 'round? You think his stupid little shop could make all that money?

SAM: Stupid little shop? Don't be ridiculous. Would you call my store a stupid little shop, Wayne? And in any case, what would she, or any one else for that matter, know about what my shop makes or doesn't make? What could she know about my many investments and other sources of income?

CYNTHIA: I know you dealing drugs. You know you dealing drugs, and anybody else who want to know only have to open their own two eyes and see.

SAM: Utter nonsense.

CYNTHIA: You dealing drugs! He's a stinking, nasty, dirty drug dealer, Wayne, and you could tell de world me, Cynthia Corbette, tell you so.

WAYNE: Look, come with me. Come let's go inside.

CYNTHIA: And you want to hear something else? I just gee
            him back his $200. Ley him tek it and stuff it.

WAYNE: Come let's go dance.

CYNTHIA: No, man, me no finish with him yet.

WAYNE: No, Cynthia. Come with me.

CYNTHIA: Me safe, Wayne.

SAM: You're right, Wayne, go dance with her.

CYNTHIA: Stinking, dutty, drugs dealer! How they let you in
            here, eh? How they let you loose among decent
            people?

WAYNE: Come, let's go, Cynthia.

CYNTHIA: Me a'right, Wayne, believe me.

WAYNE: You believe he did what you said to Roger?

CYNTHIA: He did it yes.

WAYNE: You believe he dealing drugs?

CYNTHIA: Of course, he dealing drugs. Stinking, dutty drugs
            dealer. Murderer!

WAYNE: Then what you want to be out here with him for?
            Why you even want to be in his company?

CYNTHIA: Me no done tell him all I have to say yet, man.

SAM: Well, I'm through listening to your damn non-
            sense. Pay no attention to rubbish and idle gossip,
            Wayne. You're a smart boy. Smart enough, I
            think, to see for yourself. So come by my home
            tomorrow afternoon as planned and see for your-
            self.

CYNTHIA: You going by his house tomorrow?

WAYNE: Well, he invited me, yes.

CYNTHIA: Don't go, Wayne. If you don't want what happen
             to Roger to happen to you, don't go.

SAM: More rubbish and idle gossip.

CYNTHIA: Don't go, Wayne, don't ever let this evil snake get
             close to you.

SAM: Well, Wayne, you can choose to listen to this
             rubbish or to see about your future. It's a matter
             entirely up to you.

             [Tony enters]

TONY: Still trying to steal my girl, eh, Sam?

SAM: Well, to be perfectly honest with you, yes, but
             she's a bit to much for me.

CYNTHIA: You better believe that.

WAYNE: Look, you coming with me?

CYNTHIA: It's alright now, man. Everything safe now. Come
             back for me when it's time. Alright?

             [Wayne withdraws]

TONY: Too much for you, eh?

SAM: That's right. She's all yours.

TONY: I should hope so. But, don't give up. Plenty angels
             in Heaven tonight. You could try your luck inside.

SAM: No thanks. There's only one angel for me and you
             have her already.

CYNTHIA: Two's company and three's a crowd.

SAM: Trying to tell me something, dear?

CYNTHIA: Yes. Get loss.

SAM: My, my. Well, guess I might as well. *[Heads for the exit]* Anything I can get you love birds from inside?

TONY: Nothing at all.

SAM: Take care then.

TONY: See you around, Sam.

SAM: Night, Angel.

CYNTHIA: Piss off. Creep.

              [Sam exits]

TONY: God, you got a dirty mouth.

CYNTHIA: Kiss it and make it clean. *[They kiss]* Thanks for coming back.

TONY: Anything for you, sweetheart. You know that.

CYNTHIA: Boy you should have heard me giving it to your friend, Sam Drummonds. I took him apart and threw his $200 back on him.

TONY: Good.

CYNTHIA: You should have seen me.

TONY: You didn't have to lie to me about the $200, though.

CYNTHIA: Is only because you're so touchy about these things, hon.

TONY: I don't take good enough care of you?

CYNTHIA: You know it's not that, darling.

TONY: So what is it then? Just an easy 200 bucks you couldn't pass up?

CYNTHIA: That's what you think it is?

TONY: I want you to tell me what it is.

CYNTHIA: I didn't ask him for the money, Tony. He gave it to me. He gave it to me in an envelope, so I didn't even know what it was.

TONY: You lied to me and I don't like that.

CYNTHIA: And you, of course, always tell me the truth.

TONY: You lied to me! Lied!

CYNTHIA: Oh, for Christ sake, man, if this is what you came back here for you may as well go back home to your stupid wife. *[Pause]*

TONY: Okay. If that's what you want, no problem with me. *[He starts to exit]*

CYNTHIA: Go ahead! Go right ahead for all I care.

[He leaves and she sits by herself waiting. Shortly he returns and stands up stage watching her]

TONY: You're a real bitch, you know that?

CYNTHIA: Oh, darling, don't say that. Don't even think it. *[She embraces him]*

TONY: You had no right to lie to me.

CYNTHIA: You know how you are, Tony. You would have over reacted. You would have made a mountain out of a mole hill, just as you're doing now.

TONY: I would have done no such thing.

CYNTHIA: Sure you would. You would have wanted to know
             what I did, what I said to him, how I looked at him,
             to give him the impression that I'm available for
             $200?

TONY: Well, now that you mention it, what did you do?
             What did you say to him? How did you look at him
             to give him the impression that you are available?

CYNTHIA: God! You see what I mean?

TONY: You see? You don't even know when I'm joking.
             Come here. *[He kisses her]*

             *[Dilys enter. She see what is happening, but doesn't
             want to see; doesn't want to believe]*

DILYS: *[To herself]* No! Oh, God, no, no, no! *[She retreats
             to shadows]*

CYNTHIA: Am I forgiven?

TONY: Not yet. You have to do some more penance first.

CYNTHIA: Goodie. Let's go dance.

TONY: Let's cut out from here instead.

CYNTHIA: But I want to wait until they announce the
             winners of the contest. Please? It should be any
             minute now and then we can leave right after that,
             okay?

TONY: *[Resignedly]* Whatever you sáy, I'm all yours.

CYNTHIA: No wonder I love you so much. *[They kiss passion-
             ately]* I'll go hurry them up.

TONY: Do that. And Cynthia, make it quick.

CYNTHIA: Naught boy. *[She exits. He chuckles. Long pause]*

DILYS: *[Coming out of shadows]* Tony.

TONY: Hey...Dilys? What the...what you doing back here?

DILYS: How could you Tony? How could you, man?

TONY: What you talking about?

DILYS: How could you humiliate me like this? How could you?

TONY: Dilys...look...I don't have a clue what you're talking about.

DILYS: This is the urgent call you had to make to London? That you had to make tonight because London is five hours ahead and you had to catch your client before he flew off to New York? That you had to make from your office because you didn't have the number at home? This is it? Oh, God no. *[She Cries]*

TONY: Come on, Dilys, get a hold of yourself.

DILYS: How long you been feeding me this kind of crap, Tony?

TONY: Dilys...Dilys...

DILYS: How long?

TONY: Listen, Dilys. Let me explain it to you.

DILYS: Go ahead and explain it.

TONY: Well...you see...

DILYS: I don't see.

                [Cynthia returns]

TONY: Look, Dilys...

DILYS: Explain how you could dump me on our anniversary night to be in the arms of...this!

CYNTHIA: This what?

DILYS: This slut here. Yes! This little slut.

CYNTHIA: Look, who de hell you calling a slut you stupid old cow? Who you...

TONY: Cynthia! Shut up!

DILYS: Come on, Tony we're going home. *[She takes his arm]*

CYNTHIA: *[Taking the other arm]* You not going any place, Tony. You staying right here.

DILYS: Come ahead, Tony.

CYNTHIA: I say you staying right here.

TONY: Please...please...

DILYS: Let go my husband.

CYNTHIA: Leggo me man.

TONY: Would the two of you let go of me.

DILYS: I say you're coming home with me now.

CYNTHIA: I say he staying right here with me.

DILYS: *[Releasing him]* Listen, I'm not going to be in any tug of war for you. Forget that.

CYNTHIA: Good. Now get lost.

DILYS: You going to stand there and let her talk to me like that?

TONY: Listen, Dilys, the best place for us to deal with this
             matter is at home. Let me join you there shortly
             and we can talk it over then.

DILYS: I don't believe this. I really don't believe I'm
             hearing you right.

CYNTHIA: Let her go about her damn business and wait till
             you come home, Tony. Is jail she have you in jail?

DILYS: Make up your mind, Tony, and make it up now.
             It's either me or...this.

CYNTHIA: Go 'way. You can't see when you not welcome?

DILYS: Either you come with me now and let's try and find
             a way to patch this mess up, or stay here and
             come home to an empty house.

TONY: Don't talk nonsense.

DILYS: You may think it's nonsense. Well, don't come
             with me now, and I promise you on my mother's
             grave, when you do get home I and our three
             children will be gone. And the next time you hear
             from me will be through my lawyer asking for a
             divorce. So make your choice.

TONY: I'll meet you at home in a minute.

DILYS: No. That's not good enough.

TONY: Well, it better be good enough.

DILYS: Well, I'm telling you, Mr. Tony Thompson, that it's
             not good enough! It could never be good enough.

TONY: So what's good enough, then?

DILYS: That you come with me now. That we leave here
             together as husband and wife.

CYNTHIA: Don't even listen to her, eh Tony.

DILYS: I will not have you humiliate me further, Tony. I deserve better than that. I demand better than that. So make up your mind and make it up now.

TONY: Come on. Let's go.

              [Sam enters]

CYNTHIA: You son of a bitch. You awful son of a bitch.

TONY: Hey, she's my wife. What the hell you expect me to do?

              [She rushes off to open field]

SAM: Well spoken. *[To Dilys]:* What you doing back here?

DILYS: I came to get my husband, that's all. *[She exits]*

SAM: How's my tough buddy doing?

TONY: Sam Drummonds. Yep. I can smell your hand in this.

SAM: In what?

TONY: You put Dilys up to this, you son of a bitch!

SAM: Me? Surprise at you. I wouldn't know how to play that rough.

TONY: I ought to break your frigging neck.

SAM: Easy, Tony, take it easy. You don't want to do anything to embarrass your wife.

TONY: I'm warning you, Sam, stay away from her.

SAM: Look, if it will make you feel any better, I'll stay away from her. For the sake of our friendship I'll stay away from her. And I'll tell you why. Perspective. Perspective and priorities. I happen to believe it's better in all ways for us to be friends than to be at war…and I can see the girl is special to you. So in the best interest of business and friendship I'm going to back off and leave your girl alone. Better than that, I'm going to leave now, with you, and go home. How's that?

TONY: *[He doesn't respond but moves towards field where Cynthia is]* Cynthia. Cynthia! Be cool.

CYNTHIA: Piss off!

SAM: Let's not keep Dilys waiting. *[They start moving off]* Perspective is what's important, Tony. Perspective and priorities. Let's not lose sight of them and send our world up in smoke over nonsense. *[They both exit]*

           [Wayne enters excitedly]

WAYNE: Cynthia! Cynthia! *[Pause]* Cyn?

CYNTHIA: *[Coming back on stage]* Do not call me Cyn!

WAYNE: Come on. Come on, Cynthia, everybody calling for you! We won! You hear me? We won the contest! *[Pause]* Hey, what's wrong?

CYNTHIA: Nothing.

WAYNE: Well come, let's go. De whole place clamoring for you.

CYNTHIA: You go.

WAYNE: Without you?

CYNTHIA: Tell them I gone home.

WAYNE: No, man. It wouldn' be de same without you.

CYNTHIA: Just go ahead alone no, man.

WAYNE: What's wrong? Something happen between you and Tony?

CYNTHIA: I just wish de world would open and swallow me.

WAYNE: What he did you?

CYNTHIA: He hurt me, man. He hurt me bad.

WAYNE: He hit you?

CYNTHIA: No.

WAYNE: You never listen to me, do you?

CYNTHIA: Ah wonder if he think am goin' let him get way with it?

WAYNE: What he did you?

CYNTHIA: Ah wonder if he really think so?

WAYNE: Let's go get our first prize. It will make you feel better.

CYNTHIA: Ah goin' find a way to hurt him back.

WAYNE: Just forget him.

CYNTHIA: Ah goin' hurt him so bad, he will wish he never once messed with me.

WAYNE: What you goin' do? Look, Cynthia, just forget him. Forget him as you should have done from day one. As you should have done before you ever got involved with him. Put him out of your life and keep him out.

CYNTHIA: Put him out and keep him out, yes. But ah goin' hurt him too.

            [Sam enters]

SAM: Look, they're getting on crazy for the two of you in
              there.

WAYNE: Come on Cynthia, let's go.

CYNTHIA: Ah really can't face anybody now.

WAYNE: You could handle it, man.

CYNTHIA: No. Go without me Wayne, please.

WAYNE: Okay, see you later then. *[He rushes off]*

SAM: I brought you a rum and coke. *[Pause]* You look
              like you need it.

CYNTHIA: You're damn right. *[She drinks all of it]*

SAM: I also have something else that belongs to you.

CYNTHIA: What's that?

SAM: *[Producing the $200]* This. Take it and buy your-
              self something nice to celebrate.

CYNTHIA: Celebrate what?

SAM: What I hope will be a wonderful friendship be-
              tween the two of us.

CYNTHIA: *[Taking the money]* I see.

SAM: And, if there's anything I could ever do to help,
              anything, don't hesitate to call. Enjoy the rest of
              the night. *[He starts to exit]*

CYNTHIA: Er...Mr. Drummonds...

SAM: Sam.

CYNTHIA: Sam. Is your wine nicely chilled?

SAM: The white is perfectly chilled. Red is at room temperature, as it should be.

CYNTHIA: And how's the music?

SAM: Anything you want from Arrow to Tchaikovsky.

CYNTHIA: And what's for breakfast?

SAM: Name it and you will have it. *[He tries to embrace her but she doesn't let him]*

CYNTHIA: There's only one problem. I don't want to be coaxed, or forced or tricked into anything.

SAM: Absolutely.

CYNTHIA: If you can accept those terms I'll be your guest for the night, what's left of it.

SAM: I'll tell you what, you can even have it whatever way you want. If everything is not to your liking you could leave tomorrow and never come back again. If you like, and so desire, you can let my house be your house. Come whenever you like.

CYNTHIA: We'll see.

SAM: Well, I'm ready whenever you are. *[Wayne enters]*

WAYNE: *[To Cynthia]:* You okay?

CYNTHIA: Yeah, I guess.

SAM: She couldn't be better. And congratulations.

WAYNE: Thank you. *[To Cynthia]* Here's your half of the prize money.

CYNTHIA: Keep it.

WAYNE: No way. You earned it, you keep it.

CYNTHIA: I'm giving it to you dumb, dumb.

WAYNE: Well, I'm through accepting charity tonight.

CYNTHIA: My contribution to your last year of school. A sort
              of loan. If you don't pass all your subjects you pay
              me back. Hell, no. You doan pass, I come hound-
              ing you for my 100 bucks.

WAYNE: Consider your money dead.

SAM: I'll get the car.

CYNTHIA: Okay. *[Sam Exits]*

WAYNE: Car? Wha' car. Wha' he mean he going for the car?

CYNTHIA: What you think?

WAYNE: You going with him?

CYNTHIA: He taking me home, Wayne.

WAYNE: To your home?

CYNTHIA: You have to ask?

WAYNE: Yes.

CYNTHIA: Well...actually...no. To his home.

WAYNE: You not serious.

CYNTHIA: I am.

WAYNE: Don't do it, Cynthia.

CYNTHIA: Why?

WAYNE: Because...well...

CYNTHIA: And please doan tell me to protect my good name,
            or my virtue, or because it don't look good, or any
            of that crap.

WAYNE: Alright I wouldn't tell you that. I'm just asking you
            not to do it.

CYNTHIA: For you, right?

WAYNE: Yes, for me.

CYNTHIA: Well, you out of luck. I'm through doing things for
            you tonight.

WAYNE: Do it because he's a stinking, dutty, drugs dealer
            and he can't be good for you.

CYNTHIA: My mind done mek up an' me nar change it.

WAYNE: Those are your own words, Cynthia: A stinking,
            dutty drugs dealer.

CYNTHIA: I'm going home with him, Wayne.

WAYNE: Murderer!

CYNTHIA: I'm not listening to you.

WAYNE: Murderer! *[Pause]*

CYNTHIA: You still going to see him tomorrow?

WAYNE: Why?

CYNTHIA: Just asking.

WAYNE: So you can be gone by the time I get there? Or so
            you can be all set to entertain me, as mistress of
            the manor?

CYNTHIA: For chrissake, man, is just a simple question!
            What he want you to come to his house for,
            anyway? Wha' he promise you?

WAYNE: Well, he promise to send me to med-school...in grand style. He wants to guide me and hopes we will become business partners. And...er...if this happens he promise he would make me more money than if I had a press to print it myself.

CYNTHIA: Tempted?

WAYNE: Of course I'm tempted.

CYNTHIA: And?

WAYNE: What you think?

CYNTHIA: You have to decide.

WAYNE: No, no. Tell me what you think I should do.

CYNTHIA: I can't decide for you, Wayne.

WAYNE: I'm not asking you to decide for me. I'm asking what you want me to do.

CYNTHIA: Well, don't ask me that.

WAYNE: You want what happen to Roger, or worse, to happen to me? Is that what you want, Cynthia?

CYNTHIA: Look! Do whatever you think is best for you. I'm looking out for myself. That's what I'm doing, for a change. *[Pause]* I've been used, abused, and manipulated...

WAYNE: And you just setting up yourself to be used, abused, and manipulated all over again.

CYNTHIA: No, not again. Not this time around. This time I'm looking out for me.

WAYNE: Looking out for you how?

CYNTHIA: Me Cynthia Corbette. Some kind of happiness must be out there for me too. All I want is a little bit of happiness.

WAYNE: With Sam Drummonds?

CYNTHIA: With whoever. My luck with him can't get any worse.

WAYNE: What happen with you and Tony tonight?

CYNTHIA: Don't even call his name to me, okay? Just tell yourself that over and done with. This is a new Cynthia you talking to and my new motto is do unto others before they do unto me. That's my key to happiness.

WAYNE: You doan listen to me enough, Cynthia.

CYNTHIA: And am not listening to your objections to this either. Come, I'll let Sam give you a ride home.

WAYNE: Thanks, but no thanks.

CYNTHIA: It's late. You going have a hard time getting a ride now.

WAYNE: I'll make my own way.

CYNTHIA: It's too far.

WAYNE: I'll make my own way.

CYNTHIA: As you wish.

[She exits. Wayne turns on his tape recorder. A mournful tune is heard and he starts to work out a choreography. Cynthia returns and watches for a while]

CYNTHIA: All four of Sam's tires are slashed. You wouldn't know anything about that would you?

WAYNE: Moi?

CYNTHIA: Yes you, Wayne Cabey. *[He continues to dance. Cynthia takes off the music]* I'm talking to you, man. Did you cut de man's tires?

WAYNE: You never listen to me. And I couldn't very well let him take you home now, could I?

CYNTHIA: How you know he was goin' take me home?

WAYNE: He told me. He said he understands people and he was one hundred percent certain he would take you home tonight.

CYNTHIA: He did?

WAYNE: I said no way. He said wait and see. He said I was young and innocent. That I still had a lot to learn about human nature and about women in particular. So just in case he was right I had to make it hard for him.

CYNTHIA: What's to stop me from going with him still?

WAYNE: I doan know, but I'll find something. I just hope you come to your senses before I have to start getting drastic.

CYNTHIA: He's not stupid, he's going to know who cut his tires.

WAYNE: Big deal.

CYNTHIA: And what about med-school?

WAYNE: I'll get to med-school.

CYNTHIA: All four tires. You'll do anything to stop me going home with Sam?

WAYNE: Just about anything, yes. I love you and I just
            don't want to see you getting messed up with Sam
            Drummonds. *[Long pause]*

CYNTHIA: You always look out for me, don't you. You're the
            only man I know who always look out for me, just
            for *me*. And still sometimes I treat you like dirt.

WAYNE: You just don't listen to me enough, that's all

CYNTHIA: Well, I'm going to have to start changing that.

WAYNE;   Do that. And whatever else you do, don't go getting
            sentimental on me now. Okay? Come check this
            out. *[He switches back on the music]*

CYNTHIA: You have a part for me?

WAYNE: Sure. Listen, feel it, and join in when you're ready.

            *[She joins him and they dance together, growing
            more and more into it and loosing themselves in the
            dance. Sam enters and watches. He applauds
            wildly]*

SAM: Fantastic!

WAYNE: You like it, Sam?

SAM: Out of this world. *[To Cynthia]* Ready? I managed
            to get a taxi. He's waiting for us.

CYNTHIA: I changed my mind, Sam. I'm staying with Wayne.

SAM: Oh. Why don't you both come along?

WAYNE: Thanks, but no thanks.

SAM: Really, it would be no problem at all.

WAYNE: No problem for you, maybe, but a definite problem
            for me. You see, Sam, Sam Drummonds, I'm
            simply not going your way. And just in case you

still hoping to send me to school, let me tell you as plain as I could: I'm not going to be involved with you. Not now, not ever. Not even if it would make me the richest man on earth. Not even if it's the only chance I have of making it through med school.

SAM: You're a damn ass. That's all you are. And I suspect that's all you'll ever be.

WAYNE: I sure hope you're right.

SAM: Sure you don't want to come with me, Cynthia?

CYNTHIA: Quite sure.

SAM: Well, you know how to find me. Call any time. I'll be waiting.

CYNTHIA: Don't hold your breath.

SAM: Oh, you'll come, pretty little girl. Take my word for it, sooner or later you'll come. In the meantime, Wayne, try and take good care of her. *[He starts to exist]* By the way, Wayne you wouldn't happen to know how all four of my tires managed to get slashed tonight?

WAYNE: I have a pretty good idea.

SAM: Thought you would.

WAYNE: Some man who intends to put a spoke in your wheel, who intends to slow you down, took a big knife and cut your tires.

SAM: *[Laughing]*Well, what the hell, maybe there's hope for you yet. Maybe there is. Look, call me some time. Better yet, drop by and see me. Both of you. *[He exits]*

CYNTHIA: My God, Wayne, all four of the man tires? Two
            woulda been more than enough, you devil. *[They
            embrace warmly. He lifts and spins her]*

WAYNE: Want to take it from the top again?

CYNTHIA: You doan see is morning?

WAYNE: So?

CYNTHIA: Well, why not?

            *[He fidgets with the tape recorder. The music
            comes up and they dance as the lights fade to
            black]*

THE END

Making It

(Originally titled: *Sonuvabitch)*

For Betty

Making It was first produced with the title: ***Sonuvabith***, by The Black Theatre Workshop of Montreal. It opened at the Review Theatre, Montreal, on June 4, 1975, under the direction of Arliegh Peterson, with the following cast:

MRS. PEEBLES	Cynthia Murray
STANLEY BARTEN	Charles Cobb
LINTON GUMBS	Leon St. Martin
IRMA PEEBLES	Elizabeth Armony
GEORGE O'BRIEN	Ken Pilgrim
MILDRED SWEENEY	Jacintha Thomas
SARAH	Yvette Thomas
RUSSIA BLOOD	David Edgecombe
YOUNG BLOOD	Tyrone Foster

Characters

MRS. PEEBLES, *A widow in her early fifties*

STANLEY BARTEN, *A young plantation owner*

LINTON GUMBS, *A Senior Civil Servant, about 35*

IRMA PEEBLES, *The daughter of Mrs. Peebles*

GEORGE O'BRIEN, *A young and ambitious builder*

MILDRED SWEENEY, *George's girlfriend*

SARAH, *The Peebles' maid*

RUSSIA BLOOD, *A hoodlum*

YOUNG BLOOD, *Russia Blood's son, about 10*

Setting

The play is set on a Caribbean island during the mid nineteen sixties. There are four playing areas:

1

The back verandah of the Peebles's newly built house.

(In the original production the set was designed with the verandah at stage level and the audience as the garden).

Up Right of Center is an entrance which leads from the house onto the verandah. Left, an entrance which leads to the garage. And a third entrance from the auditorium or garden area. On the veranda are a table, two chairs and a love seat.

2

The street

A ramp in front of the stage at a level just below the stage.

3

The restaurant

Down right, at its own level, is a third area which becomes the restaurant in Act One and Mildred's bedroom in Act Two. A step leads up from the ramp into this area. Two small tables each with two chairs. At the back an exit to the interior of the restaurant (back stage)

4

Mildred's bedroom

A bed along with a small dresser or side table The one entrance is from back stage.

The set should be designed to make it possible for the action of the play to be continuous.

ACT ONE

<u>**SCENE I**</u>

[The Peebles' back veranda. Music is heard as well as other sound effects which tell us a party is in progress. It is certainly not a swinging teenage or carnival type of party. Rather, it is of a more subdued and perhaps pretentious nature. Presently, Mrs. Peebles enters from house, followed by Stanley Barten]

MRS. P: …And this is the veranda.

STANLEY: It's beautiful!

MRS. P: I especially had it turned to the west so that I could sit here at afternoons and watch the sun go down.

STANLEY: Really a very good idea. It's such a wonderful view.

Mrs. P: *[In full agreement]* Isn't it. The Governor himself told me it's the best view he has ever seen.

STANLEY: Did he really?

MRS. P: He certainly did. And the view from the yard is just as lovely you know. Come and see for yourself. *[He takes in the view]*

MRS. P: Well, what do you think?

[*He turns to examine the house and then says with admiration*]Beautiful! I have to hand it to you Mrs. Peebles you've done a great job. The house is just marvellous.

MRS. P: Oh, just wait until my flowers start to blossom. Then you will see how beautiful it is. My only regret is that Mr. P. isn't here to enjoy it now it's finished.

STANLEY: That is indeed a pity. But yet, it makes what you have done even more remarkable. How many other women would have had the strength to continue after suffering such a great loss? Even in his grave he must be very proud of you.

MRS. P: That's the nicest thing I've heard in ages. You wouldn't believe the strain I've had with it. Not a single soul to give me a hand...except Irma of course.

STANLEY: Oh, I can imagine what it was like.

MRS. P: You know, once upon a time people would be glad to do something for you for nothing. Now a days if they lift a straw, they want money. All they think about is money.

STANLEY: That is perfectly true. I was never more surprised than when I got back from Cambridge. I asked one of the boys around the place to pick some coconuts and he said it would cost me two dollars. So I said, well, pick a few for me and keep three or four for yourself, and would you believe he informed me that he doesn't drink coconut water!

MRS. P: You see what I'm telling you then. And your father was such a nice man. Those people used to pick all of his fruits, tie their cattle on his land and he wouldn't do them a thing. Now they think it hard to pick two coconuts for you.

STANLEY: I was amazed. Before I went to England, a boy
            would be happy to pick a few coconuts, not just for
            me, but for almost anyone.

MRS. P: They knew their place in those days. Now every-
            body is an upstart. Take the same fellow George
            O'Brien who your father picked up from the
            gutter, for example. He put me through hell and
            high water to build this house.

STANLEY: George O'Brien built this house?

MRS. P: The boy nearly gave me a nervous breakdown.

STANLEY: You're fooling me.

MRS. P: He gave me the time of my life I'm telling you.

STANLEY: Was he actually the builder or did he just work on
            it?

MRS. P: If it was up to me, he would have never come near
            the house in the first place. But out of the
            goodness of his heart Mr. P gave him the job,
            figuring that as he was young and fighting to
            make it, it would help him out. Mr. P was like that
            you know. No wonder they walked all over him.

STANLEY: Well, well, well, I can't get over it.

MRS. P: And you would expect that if you went out of your
            way to help out somebody, that person would be
            considerate with you. Wouldn't you?

STANLEY: Certainly.

MRS. P: Any God-fearing person would be. But the Lord no
            sooner shut my husband's eyes than that brute
            turn around and want to take advantage of me.
            But he didn't know who he was dealing with.

STANLEY: I'm glad you were able to handle him. He and I started grammar school in the same year, you know. What a trouble-maker! I'm surprised he hasn't ended up in jail.

MRS. P: He's bound to end up there sooner or later. Forty-five thousand dollars I'm paying him, and you would think the house is his. If I want to change the slightest thing, it's a big offence and I still have to pay more money. Every minute is money, money and more money. The man is a criminal!

              [Irma enters from the house followed by Linton]

IRMA: Mother! How come you are sitting out here while all the guests are inside asking for you?

MRS. P: I'll be back with them in a while. Stanley and I were just having a little chat.

STANLEY: Irma! *[He comes towards her, eyes wide with admiration]* My God, you look terrific!

IRMA: Why, thank you.

LINTON: *[To Mrs. Peebles]* So that's why you can't be found...

MRS. P: Oh, Linton, I didn't know you were here already.

LINTON: This man Stanley has you monopolized. *[He shakes Stanley's hand]* How's it going?

STANLEY: Jolly good. And you.

LINTON: Not bad at all. *[He goes over and kisses Mrs. Peebles]* Congrats! The house is lovely.

MRS. P: Everybody says that. The Chief Minister, the Governor, everybody.

STANLEY: *[To Irma]* I asked for you when I arrived but Mrs. Peebles said you were getting dressed. Lovely dress.

IRMA: *[Showing off her dress]* You like it?

STANLEY: It's gorgeous!

IRMA: Thank you again, sir. Linton, what's become of George?

LINTON: I don't know. Hasn't he arrived yet?

STANLEY: Who was that?

IRMA: George O'Brien.

MRS. P: He's not coming here!

IRMA: Of course he is. I invited him.

MRS. P: Here? To my house?

IRMA: No Mother, to the moon. Of course here. Where else?

MRS. P: Have you gone crazy?

IRMA: Why shouldn't he be at the house-warming party? He designed and built it didn't he?

MRS. P: He was paid, wasn't he? Because he built the house doesn't mean I have to rub shoulders with him. It doesn't mean I have to subject my guests to socializing with riff-raff!

IRMA: Oh Mother! If you could only hear yourself, I'm sure you'd be surprised to learn how ridiculous you sound.

MRS. P: You see my point Stanley?

STANLEY: Well, er...er...

IRMA: Mother! Your guests are all in...

MRS. P: *[Seeing George as he enters through the garden]* Why the hell he think he should be tramping through my garden?

IRMA: Oh, hello George.

MRS. P: Just see to it he keeps out of my way! *[She exits]*

STANLEY: Not exactly her cup of tea, is he?

LINTON: Simple case of a poor boy getting rich too fast.

IRMA: Never mind her. Come on up.

GEORGE: I thought the party's supposed to be inside?

LINTON: *[Extending a hand]* What's happening George?

GEORGE: What's happening Boss-man?

LINTON: You tell me. It's all happening with you.

GEORGE: How could you say that? *[Indifferently to Stanley]* Hi.

STANLEY: How's it going, old chap?

GEORGE: Can't complain.

STANLEY: I was remarking on the marvellous job you've done on the house. Simply marvellous!

GEORGE: Is that so?

STANLEY: Why don't you try for a scholarship to England or someplace and go away to study Architecture? With your talent you could go a long way.

GEORGE: I'll think about it.

STANLEY: Really, you should. With a degree in Architecture there'll be no stopping you. You ought to think seriously about it.

GEORGE: *[Looks at him but says nothing. Then he addresses Linton]* So, what's all the good?

LINTON: I'm just here admiring your handiwork.

STANLEY: *[To Irma]* May I have this dance?

IRMA: *[Indifferently]* Okay. *[They start to leave. To George and Linton]* Please don't forget, gentlemen, the party's inside now.

LINTON: Don't worry about that.

GEORGE: *[Watching them go]* Who he think he pulling that shit on? *[Mimicking Stanley]* "Marvellous job, ole chap. Why don't you go away to England and study?" The damn ass. Look at this house. Now tell me, does he really believe I woke up one morning, decided to build a house, knocked some cement and a few blocks together and ended up with this?

LINTON: Come on, George, the man was only trying to be friendly.

GEORGE: Friendly? How come all of a sudden he want to be friendly with me?

LINTON: What choice he has? Nobody taking them on with that high society nonsense anymore. Times are changing, that's all.

GEORGE: Times might change, but not me.

LINTON: You going hold a grudge against him all your life?

GEORGE: You forgetting that he is the same Stanley Barten who made his father kick me out of school?

LINTON: I'm not forgetting anything.

GEORGE: You have to be. *[Mimicking Stanley again]* "With
             a degree in Architecture there'll be no stopping
             you."

LINTON: Look George, you and I know that degree or no
             degree, there's still no stopping you, right?

GEORGE: Bet your life on that! *[Suddenly remembering]* I got
             the contract to build the new hotel, you know.

LINTON: No joking!

GEORGE: You have any idea how much money there is to be
             made right here in the next few years?

LINTON: What you mean if I have any idea? I'll tell you one
             thing, you sure as ass picked the right trade at the
             right time.

GEORGE: And now the gravy beginning to flow, that
             cocksucker want me to run off to university and
             leave it.

LINTON: You gone back on that nonsense again!

GEORGE: But no! That's what he want me to do in truth.
             Run away and leave everything for the white
             contractors who coming in from every place. You
             don't understand fellows like Barten, man. They
             just hate to see poor people get ahead. But I goin'
             show them.

LINTON: *[Changing the subject]* So, you really got the job to
             build the hotel? Man, that's great news!

GEORGE: It's not as good as it should be.

LINTON: Why not?

GEORGE: I have to share the job with Will Samuels.

LINTON: The Seventh Day Adventist man?

GEORGE: Same one.

LINTON: So what's wrong with that?

GEORGE: If Earl Johnson was going to get the whole loaf, why can't I get it too?

LINTON: Oh, come on...

GEORGE: Why can't I? Because I'm not white? Because I'm not from America...or because I didn't go abroad to study?

LINTON: *[Slight pause]* Look George, there's not another man on earth who would be happy as me to see you get the whole contract. But have you stopped to consider: one, the amount of money you have to raise, and two, the risk that's going to be involved?

GEORGE: If Earl Johnson could raise the money, so could I.

LINTON: Look, Johnson's white face is all the collateral he needs. What you have to show the bank?

GEORGE: If he could raise it, I could damn well raise it too.

LINTON: Maybe. But let's not deceive ourselves.

GEORGE: Sixty thousand dollars profit I could make off that hotel, I tell you. Sixty big ones.

LINTON: George, you're a builder you know, not a magician.

GEORGE: You want me to spell out for you how I can do it?

LINTON: Okay. For the sake of argument, let us suppose...

GEORGE: Suppose nothing!

LINTON: Okay. Don't get excited. Let's grant then, that you could make sixty thousand dollars in one shot. When you consider the amount of hotels and private houses that are going to go up in the next ten, fifteen years, sixty thousand dollars is just a drop in the bucket. Right or wrong?

GEORGE: Right.

LINTON: So at least we agree on one thing. Now here's what I'm saying: Why not build the hotel with Samuels and use that as a nucleus to create a firm of contractors which...

GEORGE: Not Samuels! Man, if Samuels belly hurt him twice in one week, you can't convince him that somebody not trying to work obeah on him.

LINTON: So what? All I'm saying is, with such a firm...

GEORGE: Samuels is not...

LINTON: Jesus Christ! You going let me finish?

GEORGE: Okay. Go ahead, say what you saying.

LINTON: What I'm saying is: you could use this firm of builders to monopolize the industry and control the bulk of the money.

GEORGE: Look Linton, you must realize that I didn't wake up yesterday and discover there's a lot of bread to be made. I've seen it coming for years and I know there's plenty merit in what you're saying, but Samuels and those boys are jokers, man. They're laborers!

LINTON: You know what's going to happen? While you local fellows busy cutting each others throats over the crumbs, some company from America or Canada is going to waltz in and dance away with the whole damn bread factory. You just wait and see.

GEORGE: Never happen! Not as long as I'm around.

LINTON: What move you making to prevent it?

GEORGE: Nothing stopping me from getting my share of that gravy.

LINTON: Sure you will get gravy. But I'm trying to show you that your share could be twice as big.

GEORGE: Look, setting up a firm calls for plenty of planning and organization. You can't expect me to go into something as serious as that with a dunce. If it was you now...

LINTON: But I don't know anything about building.

GEORGE: You don't have to know anything about building. You studied economics and business, here's your chance to put it to some practical use. The two of us working together could control the building industry, I'm tired telling you that.

LINTON: The offer is tempting, to tell you the truth, but you have to remember I've already given most of my life...

GEORGE: I know you have a good respectable job with government and all that, but man, there's money to be made and building is where it is. To hell with this prestige thing. *[Pause. In the silence George urges a response that is not forthcoming]* Don't tell me you're one of those brainwashed niggers who behave as if money is claps. Avoid it at all cost, and if you happen to get a dose, party day and night until you get rid of it! Is that your philosophy too? You ain't tired of being poor, man.

LINTON: Sure we can make a lot of money together, but man cannot live by bread alone. You're asking me to turn my back on a profession I've given some of the best years of my life to.

GEORGE: Oh shit!

LINTON: I'm not as young as I used to be, you know!

GEORGE: You're getting soft, Linton.

LINTON: Maybe, but you have to put yourself in my position.

GEORGE: My position is this: wherever you find the money, that's where you find me.

LINTON: Listen...and this is strictly confidential. In the next few weeks I'm going to become a Permanent Secretary to a different Ministry.

GEORGE: *[Sarcastically]* So?

LINTON: Get this: Permanent Secretary to the Ministry of Real Estate and Construction! You see what that could mean? *[Pause]*

GEORGE: *[Smiling]* Now you beginning to make sense. You going to have a big say in who builds what and who builds where?

LINTON: Exactly. If we both look after each other's interest we could both do pretty well.

GEORGE: I see what you're saying but I still think you're just playing it safe.

            [Irma enters]

IRMA: Just look at the two of you gossiping out here while the party is swinging inside. Come here Linton.

LINTON: At your service. *[She takes him by the arm and propels him inside]*

IRMA: In you go! Go dance or have a drink or something.

LINTON:	You're sure you want to let me loose in your bar!
IRMA:	Keep going.
LINTON:	*[As he goes offstage]* I'll bring you a drink, George.
IRMA:	*[Turning and walking slowly towards George]* Well, Mr. O'Brien?
GEORGE:	Well, Miss Peebles?
IRMA:	I've been waiting to get you by yourself all night.
GEORGE:	Is that so?
IRMA:	I have a very important question to ask you.
GEORGE:	Go ahead.
IRMA:	What exactly is going on between you and Mildred Sweeney?
GEORGE:	Look, you mean to tell me you interrupt such a good conversation to ask me nonsense like this?
IRMA:	How could it be nonsense when every place I go people telling me you're planning to get married to her?
GEORGE:	Well, if you want to go around believing everything people tell you, that's up to you.
IRMA:	Is it true or not?
GEORGE:	Look Irma, if I ever decide to get married, you'd be the first to know, okay?
IRMA:	You're avoiding the question, George! Give me a straight answer. Is it true or not?
GEORGE:	Eh, eh. You sound as if you want to fight me?

IRMA: I'm asking you a simple question, George. Are you planning to marry Mildred or not?

GEORGE: Well, I never see…Look, get one thing straight. I'm my own man. I do whatever I like and I don't have to answer to you or anyone else. Try and remember that.

IRMA: So that's how it is. Now you finish using me you want to carry on as you like with another woman and I mustn't ask you about it?

GEORGE: Use you?

IRMA: Yes! That's exactly what I said.

GEORGE: Don't get me mad tonight, woman.

IRMA: Get mad all you want! It's still me who pleaded and begged my father to give you the job to build this house! And now you finish stuffing your pockets with my money, you want to walk out on me as if I don't exist.

GEORGE: Wait a minute! Ley we get down to the facts right now! The only reason your father gave me the job to build this house is because I built it for two thousand dollars less than any other contractor in the land would even touch it for!

IRMA: That's a lie!

GEORGE: You could have pleaded and begged from now until kingdom come, if he could have gotten it built elsewhere for a cent less, I would never have gotten the job.

IRMA: That's not true!

GEORGE: That's a fact! And you damn well know it! So don't come handing me no shit about using you, you spoilt bitch! *[She fires a vicious slap at him, but he catches her hand in mid-air, twists it hard behind her back and pushes her away]* Don't let me have to break your frigging hand tonight.

IRMA: *[Stunned by this response, she says in a whimpering voice]* You hurt me. You realize that? You nearly broke my arm.

GEORGE: Shit! You lucky. That's what I should have done.

IRMA: Stinking dog!

GEORGE: *[Mimicking her]* Stinking dog! What gives you the right to slap me? Whenever you hear the truth you become vicious? Well, here's something else you're not going to like.

IRMA: *[Covering her ears]* I don't want to hear anything!

GEORGE: Next time you want to slap somebody, make sure you could afford it. Law suits cost plenty money these days and your family doesn't have it any more.

IRMA: How could we, after you finish robbing us down?

GEORGE: Robbing you down!

IRMA: Don't try to pretend you're above that.

GEORGE: Don't get me wrong sweetheart. Sure I'd rob you, if you and your mother hadn't squandered all of whatever little there was to rob. You have any idea how big a mortgage is on this house?

IRMA: The financial affairs of my family is none of your concern.

GEORGE: You're right. It's none of my concern. But if you want to run around being a heavy, you better start making it more of your concern. And you could pass the word on to your mother.

IRMA: So it's Mommy you're after! Well, why are you chewing me out? I'm tired telling you, George, Mother is not me. Even tonight when you twisted my arm, I hardly made a sound. You know what would have happened if I had gone inside and raised a fuss?

GEORGE: No. Tell me.

IRMA: Think about it.

GEORGE: Your mother would send for the British Army to hang me?

IRMA: Very funny! She'd make things in this land so hard for you, you'd dig a hole and beg somebody to bury you.

             [Half-way through the next speech, Linton enters with a drink for George]

GEORGE: Don't make me laugh. Pomp and prestige can't pass for power anymore, my dear. Today it takes money, M-O-N-E-Y, money.

LINTON: Okay professor, have a drink and give your tongue a rest.

IRMA: It's a good thing you came back, Linton. Your friend here was threatening to break all the bones in my body.

LINTON: I forgot to warn you. You have to be careful with him. His affections have a way of getting out of control.

IRMA: His affections? Unless of course you mean his love for money.

LINTON: *[Jokingly]* He does have quite a fondness for money, doesn't he?

IRMA: 'Quite' is not the word. Though what he'll do with it only heaven knows. He's certainly too…He certainly wouldn't understand how to appreciate the finer delicacies of life.

LINTON: Okay, let's not get nasty.

IRMA: Nasty? You should have heard some of the things he said to me. It's not possible to be any nastier than he is.

MRS. P: *[She enters with Stanley]* Linton, have you seen…ah! There she is! What are you doing here? Stanley has been looking all over for you. Is something wrong?

IRMA: Nothing is wrong, Mother.

MRS. P: You'd better take her in out of the cold air for a while, Stanley.

STANLEY: That sounds like a jolly good idea to me. *[They exit]*

MRS. P: *[Taking hold of Linton]* Come and say hello to the rest of the guests, Linton. *[They move off. She pauses]* Oh, O'Brien, there's something in the bathroom I want you to…

GEORGE: *[Cutting her off]* If there's something else you want done, Mrs. Peebles, come to my office tomorrow or phone me there.

MRS. P: Are you trying to tell me that you can't even take a little…

GEORGE: I'm only trying to tell you that I didn't come here to work. *[Mrs. Peebles is beginning to become very annoyed. Before she explodes, Linton cuts in]*

LINTON: Okay, Mrs. Peebles. You go back inside and let me talk to him.

MRS. P: Alright, Linton, if you say so. *[She exits]*

GEORGE: Before you open your mouth to say anything, let me tell you flat, I'm not looking at a thing for that woman tonight.

LINTON: Relax it, George, relax it. What harm is it to you to look at what she's showing you?

GEORGE: I bet you she doesn't have anything to show me. She just figures I shouldn't be here, that's all.

LINTON: Fine. You know that, so let her feel how she wants to feel. You don't have to let her know that she's annoying you.

GEORGE: So you want me to be a hypocrite then?

LINTON: I want you to be diplomatic, man!

GEORGE: What the hell's the difference? *[Pause]*

LINTON: Have you heard about kissing the fool and letting it pass?

GEORGE: Do you have any idea how much shit I've taken from that fool over the past few months?

LINTON: Is me you telling about shit-taking, man? How you think I got to where I am? All we have to do is play our cards right, George, just play them right, and the asses we're kissing today we can turn around and kick tomorrow!

GEORGE: *[Laughing]* I don't know why I still bother to argue with you sometimes. But I still not looking at any bathroom tonight.

LINTON: Well , if you don't want to look at it, don't look at it. What the hell! *[They start to leave down left through the garden which spills down into the auditorium]* Let's go down to the club and I'll buy you one.

GEORGE: *[Considering the offer]* Ah, maybe just one. *[They leave as Irma enters followed by Stanley]*

STANLEY: By golly, you disappear quickly. I couldn't imagine where on earth you could have got to after that last dance. Have you been hiding from me?

IRMA: No. I haven't been hiding. *[She sits in love seat]*

STANLEY: Having a good time?

IRMA: Sure!

STANLEY: Would you like a drink?

IRMA: No thank you.

STANLEY: Shall we dance again?

IRMA: No, not this one.

STANLEY: Is anything the matter? If that O'Brien...

IRMA: If that O'Brien what? I told you I'm fine.

STANLEY: Okay, okay...If you say so. *[An awkward pause. He gets up and looks at the sky]* It's such a beautiful night, a night for lovers, don't you think?

IRMA: It's not bad.

STANLEY: Wouldn't it be nice if people could control love? Dictate the direction of its flow?

IRMA: What you mean?

STANLEY: Well, be able to love only those who would return your love with equal strength. It would destroy the deadly unbalance which brings so much pain to so many millions. Don't you agree?

IRMA: I suppose so. *[An uncomfortable silence. We see it torturing him. Suddenly pent up frustrations demand a voice]*

STANLEY: What's the matter Irma? Why can't I ever reach you? From ever since I got back from England I've been trying to make contact with you, but...but...

IRMA: But what?

STANLEY: There is this invisible wall of ice around you which, try as I may, I can't get by. Why is it so hard for us to try to relate to each other?

IRMA: I don't know. *[She gets up and walks away from him. Pause]*

STANLEY: Is it because there's someone else?

IRMA: Let's not get into that.

STANLEY: I would really like to know, Irma. Is there?

IRMA: Why do you want to know?

STANLEY: I just want to know. Is there someone else?

IRMA: Look, please...

STANLEY: Is there?

IRMA: *[Angrily]* Yes! There is!

STANLEY: *[Wounded]* Irma. *[He takes her hand to lead her back to the love seat but she is stiff]* Irma, will you sit down again? Please?

IRMA: *[Allowing him to lead her back]* What is it now?

STANLEY: Could we...could we talk about it?

IRMA: I don't want to talk about it, okay?

[Mrs. Peebles enters]

MRS. P: Is everything okay? Good. It's really nice to see both of you getting along so well together. Where's that O'Brien?

STANLEY: I think he may have left.

MRS. P: Linton must have dragged him off. Just as well. He shouldn't have been here in the first place

IRMA: Oh, for heaven…!

MRS. P: He had no right to be here, Irma! No right at all. It's as simple as that! He doesn't belong here. But, please, let's not argue about it. Take good care of this guest, while I go inside and look after all our other guests. Do continue enjoying yourself, Stanley, dear.

            [She exits. Lights go out quickly. A short music bridge leads into Scene II]

SCENE II

[On the street the next day. The lights come up on George and Mildred. He is helping her with a bag of groceries]

MILDRED: I have to go now, George. But I'll meet you tonight at the restaurant. *[She reaches for the bag, he draws away]*

GEORGE: Why you doan let me come home with you?

MILDRED: Mama is waiting on me, George, and you know how funny she could be.

GEORGE: Is time you stop being afraid of your mother, you know. *[Pause]* By the way, why she didn't let you come last night?

MILDRED: She's been getting on very funny.

GEORGE: About us?

MILDRED: Yes.

GEORGE: Funny in what way?

MILDRED: You know. Asking stupid questions like...like when you going to give your heart to God and so on.

GEORGE: Give my heart to God? What the devil nonsense is this? Tell her He has my heart. He has the whole of me. *[Pause]* What she mean is when I'm going to become a Seventh Day Adventist?

MILDRED: I guess so.

GEORGE: How come all of a sudden your mother so dead set against me?

MILDRED: She's not really against you. It's just that...well...look George, I really have to go now, I'll tell you later.

GEORGE: No, no. Tell me now. *[Pause]* Go ahead, tell me now.

MILDRED: It's just that...well...this man, Will Samuels, has written to her asking her for me...

GEORGE: To marry you? I didn't know people still doing that nonsense anymore. How come you didn't tell me before?

MILDRED: Is nothing George.

GEORGE: Nothing!

MILDRED: Brother Will is almost twice my age. What am I going to do with him?

GEORGE: And your mother?

MILDRED: She feels he's in the church, so...She's an old-fashioned woman and these things mean a lot to her.

GEORGE: Look, I'm coming home with you now. It's time me and your parents had a serious talk.

MILDRED: No George! You want them to kill me?

GEORGE: Kill you?

MILDRED: They not expecting you and they will feel I just brought you home like that.

GEORGE: So what?

MILDRED: Please, George, don't come now. Let me go home first and tell them you want to see them. Please.

[Sarah enters]

SARAH: Mildred! Me just coming to look for you, girl. You mother up there waiting on you.

GEORGE: Alright, do that. Tell them I'm coming to speak with them tomorrow. I'll see you at the restaurant later.

MILDRED: Okay, George. *[He exits left]* She vex?

SARAH: Not really. She only say she sure is down by George O'Brien you is.

MILDRED: And she not vex?

SARAH: Girl, if you know what good for you, you would rest that man right at the foot o' de cross.

MILDRED: What all of you trying to poison my mind against the fellow for?

SARAH: You don't know he liming Irma Peebles strong, strong?

MILDRED: Not a thing could go so.

SARAH: You forgetting wey me work. Me have to be in de know. Every minute Irma tell she mother she gone to the beach with friends. Gone where? She and George gone driving all over the place. She bad lek salt. Me hear she say wid me own two ear that George is the onlyest man for she and she going to married to him if is the last thing she do.

MILDRED: She tell you so for true?

SARAH: Faith to God!

MILDRED: She could say what she like. That don't mean the two of them in nothing.

SARAH: Is George O'Brien you putting you trust in? Gel, you getting stupid or wha?

MILDRED: What so stupid about that?

SARAH: Even you suppose to see that all he concern bout is making money and getting ahead.

MILDRED: So you vex because he fighting to make something of himself?

SARAH: I tell you, Mildred, George O'Brien don't have the slightest bit of good intention for you. Is a society woman who he feel going help him get ahead that he want. And is six months now at least he and Irma liming strong, strong.

MILDRED: And how come I don't hear nothing?

SARAH: Because they have it cover up. You think they could let Mistress Peebles find out?

MILDRED: And how come he was going to take me to the house opening last night?

SARAH: George no stupid! He know Sister Sweeney wasn't going to let you go, so he could afford to ask you anything. And if she did let you go, then you would see how fast he back down.

MILDRED: It getting late. Come we go. *[They begin to leave, right]*

SARAH: Do God bless you, Mildred, tek me advice and rest that man.

            [Lights fade. A short music bridge. Lights come up on bar]

SCENE III

[Stanley and Linton are seated in the restaurant. They each have a drink. There are two entrances: One leading to another section of the restaurant and one from the outside, which runs across the front of the stage]

STANLEY: You know, there's a comment you made last night that has been puzzling me.

LINTON: What's that?

STANLEY: It was about O'Brien. I remarked that Mrs. Peebles wasn't awfully fond of him and you said something to the effect of him being a poor man getting rich too quickly.

LINTON: That's exactly it. But it is not so much his getting rich that upsets her. She probably isn't even aware of the fact that he is sitting on a potential gold mine. What annoys her is the independence of spirit it has given him.

STANLEY: But look at you, Linton. Your parents were poor too, and you're just as independent, but she doesn't treat you like that.

STANLEY: But look at you, Linton. Your parents were poor too, and you're just as independent, but she doesn't treat you like that.

LINTON: Of course not. I go to work in a jacket and tie. There're letters behind my name, my walls are covered with certificates—my tickets to acceptance and respectability.

STANLEY: That's not how I see it Linton, that's not how I see it at all. You're just a different kind of person altogether.

LINTON: Meaning I don't rock the boat, whereas he doesn't even attempt to be nice.

STANLEY: Meaning he's not in your class. *[Linton laughs]* What's so funny?

LINTON: You reminded me of Mrs. Peebles, that's all. I find her preoccupation with class a bit ridiculous.

STANLEY: I'm not preoccupied with class.

LINTON: I never said you were. Anyway, let's forget it. How're things on the estate?

STANLEY: Well...jolly good I suppose.

LINTON: You suppose?

STANLEY: As you know, my heart isn't really fully in it as yet. You must be tired of hearing me say this, but my father died too soon. He should have held out until I had finished my doctorate.

LINTON: Go and finish it now.

STANLEY: Who'd manage the estate for me while I was away? That's my problem.

LINTON: You ever thought of selling some of that land?

LINTON: Why not? A few Americans have bought land to build rest homes. In the next few years much more of them will be wanting land, and whatever the Yankees do, the Canadians are sure to follow. The price of land is going to shoot up like a rocket. You could make a fortune.

STANLEY: My father and grandfather worshipped that estate. How can I...

LINTON: Your father and grandfather were clearly two shrewd businessmen.

STANLEY: No, no. They didn't just love the land for the wealth it brought them. They loved the earth itself; planting tiny seeds and watching them grow was a way of life, a source of peace and contentment.

LINTON: And for you?

STANLEY: It will come with time. You don't understand, Linton. The glory of that estate was drilled into me even more than the Lord's Prayer. My father's sole regret in life was that he didn't see the grandson who I would pass the land on to. You're getting the picture? Selling the land would be like selling my very soul.

LINTON: I'm not insisting that you sell the whole estate. It just occurred to me that the big money is now in real estate and if an estate like yours is not handled skilfully, it could easily prove to be more of a liability than an asset. And, after all you're my friend, I have to be concerned about your welfare.

STANLEY: I appreciate that, Linton. Really, I do. But don't worry about it. People will always have to eat, wouldn't they? I'll manage.

LINTON: That's a good point.

[George enters with notebook]

GEORGE: Hey, Linton, Russia Blood reach here yet?

LINTON: He was here earlier, asking for you. Said he'll
             come back later.

GEORGE: Good.

LINTON: You know of course management doesn't like him
             being around here?

GEORGE: Don't worry, I'll be responsible for it.

LINTON: Pull up a chair.

GEORGE: It's alright. I'm expecting company and I have to
             check something here. *[He sits by himself and
             writes in his notebook]*

STANLEY: Linton, there's something I've been meaning to
             ask you.

LINTON: Uh-huh.

STANLEY: It's a bit personal.

LINTON: That's okay.

STANLEY: Do you know if Irma is having an affair with
             anyone?

LINTON: Apart from you?

STANLEY: I haven't really been making much headway. Last
             night she told me there was a third party. You
             think it might be him?

LINTON: George? Hardly. I know they have become reason-
             ably good friends since he started the house, but
             I don't think it's more than that.

STANLEY: I can't imagine who it could be.

LINTON: I hope you're not worrying your head about it. Irma is a nice girl yes, but if the chemistry isn't working there're lots more who are available.

STANLEY: I keep telling myself that, but the truth is, my heart has anchored itself on her and I can't find strength enough to budge it.

            [Russia Blood enters]

R BLOOD: Here me is sah. *[Looking over his shoulder and shouting]* Boy, come ya! *[A boy appears. Russia Blood grabs him by the collar and drags him in]* Me no tell you fu stap close to me. Wey you manners. You no see Marse George.

BOY: Good arfnoon...

R BLOOD: Tek arf you hat, fella! Me no tired tell you foo tek arf you hat when you talk to people!

BOY: *[Pulling off hat]* Arfnoon, Marse George.

GEORGE: How you do Young Blood?

R BLOOD: 'E bad lek yaws, a tell you. I don't know wha' going become o' 'e in life. Siddown and behave yourself now. *[Boys sits]*

GEORGE: Go inside an' tell dem I say to gee you a ice-cream. *[Boy looks at father]*

R BLOOD: Go ahead. *[He exits]*

STANLEY: I'm getting out of here. Why don't you come over to the house and have supper with me?

LINTON: Sounds good to me. There's a poker game at the club later if you're interested.

STANLEY: Sure. Splendid idea. *[They start to leave]*

LINTON: *[To George]* See you around.

GEORGE: Take it easy. *[They leave]*

R BLOOD: He too feel he white, you know.

GEORGE: Give him a chance, he's a good boy. Anyway, here's what I want you to do for me. You hear that me an' Samuels going build a hotel?

R BLOOD: Me hear everything.

GEORGE: Well, this is what you have to do. Get some jumbie beads and some dead bones and sprinkle them around the site of the hotel and round Samuels' house and pick-up. You have to make him believe that somebody working obeah on him. You get me?

R BLOOD: Me got you. You want de job for you one.

GEORGE: Right.

R BLOOD: Well, why you don't let me fix him up for true and done?

GEORGE: No, no. Don't bother with that. Just make he believe somebody trying to molest him. That's all.

R BLOOD: Well, you is the boss. If that's what you want, that's what you get.

GEORGE: You have to put some the jumbie beads and so round my place too. Then about next week Friday, me want you to mash up Samuels' truck so that he can't use it for about a month; and the same night you must burn down the old shed where I keep tools and lumber. You get me?

R BLOOD: Me got you, me got you!

             [Youngblood re-enters with ice-cream]

GEORGE: Good. Look after it for me now and make sure you frighten the shit out of Samuels. Then me and you would fix up.

R BLOOD: Don't hurt your head, man. Me going look after it real good. *[Noticing boy who is busy eating ice-cream with fingers. He slaps him across the head]* Boy! Tek you finger out o' de ice-cream! You go on lek me no learn you no manners and behavior! Go ask for a spoon. *[Boy exits]*

R BLOOD: Just one more thing, boss. Dis 'lee boy o' mine coming big man fast. Is time 'e start to learn fu fen' for heself. Do me a favor and teach 'e a trade.

GEORGE: He still in school?

R BLOOD: Yes.

GEORGE: Good. Let him come on Saturday, and after school in de arfnoon. One de men will teach him something.

R BLOOD: *[To boy as he returns]* You hear that? Marse George say he-a go learn you wan trade. Say t'anks.

BOY: T'ank you, Marse George.

R BLOOD: Put you hat pon you head. Me no tell you foo keep you hat pon you head. *[He forces hat on boy's head as Irma walks in. She sneaks up behind George and covers his eyes with her hand]*

IRMA: Three guesses.

GEORGE: Cut the shit out, Irma.

IRMA: *[Taking away her hands]* Where's your sense of humor?

R BLOOD: Tell Miss Irma howdy.

BOY: Arfnoon, Miss Irma.

IRMA: Hello. You behaving yourself?

R BLOOD: 'E bad lek yaws, Miss Irma. I don't know wa' I goin'
                do wid he. *[She reaches in her purse and gives him
                a coin]* Say t'ank you.

BOY: T'ank you.

R BLOOD: T'anks who?

BOY: T'ank you, Miss Irma.

R BLOOD: Come ley we go now. [Just *before they exit]* You got
                de spoon?

BOY: *[Showing spoon]* Got it.

IRMA: You got my message?

GEORGE: Yes, but I'm going to be busy.

IRMA: You're still vexed about last night.

GEORGE: The least said about last night the better!

IRMA: I'm sorry, George, it's only because I was hurt. You
                don't hold it against me?

GEORGE: Look, Irma, why don't you call me later?

IRMA: You expecting company?

GEORGE: I told you I was going to be busy.

IRMA: What are you so busy doing?

GEORGE: Look, Irma, just don't get me vex now, okay?

IRMA: Okay, Mr. O'Brien, I can take a hint. I know when I'm not wanted. *[She gets up and sees Mildred entering. George does not see Mildred as his back is to her. Suddenly Irma falls into George's lap, throws her arms around his neck and starts to kiss him. Mildred freezes. Then she turns and runs off]*

GEORGE: What the hell was that for? Are you going crazy?

IRMA: You looked so handsome that I couldn't resist it!

GEORGE: *[Smiling in spite of himself]* You must learn to control yourself better than that. Suppose somebody saw you and tell your mother?

IRMA: I don't give a damn! I love you, George and I'm not ashamed of it. I don't care what my mother or anybody says.

GEORGE: *[Touched, he kisses her lightly]* Alright, get home safely now. I'll talk to you.

IRMA: *[Taking a few steps then turning back]* I'll wait for you in the car for a while in case your guest doesn't come and you get bored sitting here by yourself. *[She leaves. George sits alone drinking as the lights slowly fade. Short music bridge]*

<u>SCENE IV</u>

About three weeks later. The Peebles' verandah.

[Mrs. Peebles is knitting. Irma is relaxing with a book. Sarah enters with a glass of water and some pills]

SARAH: You forget to take your tablets ma'am.

               [Mrs. P. drinks the pills and gives the glass back]

               I could have the rest of the arfnoon off, Miss Jane?

MRS. P: Why should I give you the rest of the afternoon off?

SARAH: Is a wedding I have to go to, ma'am.

MRS. P: I haven't heard about any wedding.

SARAH: Is a small wedding ma'am.

MRS. P: Who is getting married?

SARAH: Mildred Sweeney, ma'am.

IRMA: *[Suddenly becoming interested]* Mildred Sweeney? Who is she getting married to?

SARAH: Will Samuels.

IRMA: *[Relieved]* Oh, that's nice. They deserve each other. How so suddenly?

SARAH: Brother Will got his papers to go to Canada next week.

IRMA: Canada? But isn't he supposed to be building the hotel with George?

SARAH: Not anymore. He say the Lord told him he should give it up and go to Canada.

IRMA: Is she going to Canada next week too?

SARAH: I don't...

MRS. P: You can have the rest of the day off if you want, but you know of course you would have to make up for it.

SARAH: Yes, ma'am.

MRS. P: I don't like dirty dishes lying around in the kitchen overnight. So make sure that after the wedding you come back here and clean up the kitchen.

SARAH: Yes, ma'am.

MRS. P: You could go 'bout your business now.

SARAH: Thank you, Miss Jane. *[She leaves, grumbling under her breath]*Clean up de kitchen, wash up de dishes, sweep out de house…

MRS. P: Irma.

IRMA: Yes, Mother.

MRS. P: You seemed awfully concerned about that wedding.

IRMA: I did?

MRS. P: And very relieved to find out that it is Samuels she is marrying and not O'Brien.

IRMA: What are you driving at, Mother?

MRS. P: I've been hearing some things about you, Irma, which I prefer to believe are not true.

IRMA: You are always hearing things about me.

MRS. P: Well, is it or isn't it true?

IRMA: How would I know? I don't know what you heard.

MRS. P: What is this business about you carrying on a love affair with that vagabond, O'Brien?

IRMA: George and I are just good friends, Mother!

MRS. P: Is O'Brien anybody for you to be good friends with?

IRMA: What do you mean? If he is my good friend, he's my good friend. You yourself have often told me that good friends are hard to come by and should be treasured.

MRS. P: Well, this is what I'm telling you now. Whatever the relationship is between you two, I want you to put an end to it immediately!

IRMA: Mother! You've already lived your life. Please don't try to live mine too.

MRS. P: It is not a subject that I wish to discuss, Irma!

IRMA: How often must I beg you not to interfere in my life?

MRS. P: I am not interfering in your life. I'm merely doing this for your own good.

IRMA: For heaven's sake, let me be the judge of what is for my own good, and pay closer attention to the things which are for your own good.

MRS. P: Don't try to evade the issue, Irma!

IRMA: Like this amount of debt you put us in for example!

MRS. P: What nonsense are you talking about?

IRMA: It isn't nonsense. We could even lose the house, Mother.

MRS. P: Let me worry about the house. That's not the issue at the moment! How can you let your name be mentioned in the same breath with George O'Brien? If there is anything at all between you two, I want you to put an immediate stop to it!

IRMA: Mother, you are not...

MRS. P: I will not stand for any arguments, Irma!

IRMA: Well, if that's the attitude you want to take, it's fine with me! *[She leaves]*

MRS. P: *[Rushing after her]* Irma! Come back here!

[*She is taken by a sudden stab of pain and clutches her breast. It quickly passes and although she is shaken, she continues to go off*]

I'm talking to you, Irma! Irma!

[*Lights fade*]

SCENE V

[*Later that night. Melancholy music is heard as the lights come up on the restaurant. George is alone drinking. He is obviously dejected. Presently Linton enters*]

LINTON: Thought I'd find you here.

[*A pause during which Linton sits. It is an awkward situation and he is trying to determine how best to deal with it*]

Been here long? [*George nods*]

The hotel coming along okay?

[*George nods again*]

GEORGE: Coming from the wedding?

LINTON: Yeah. [*Pause*] Take a holiday, George. Go some place and relax your brain.

GEORGE: My brain alright, man. Don't worry about me.

LINTON: What really happened? Both of you had a quarrel or something like that?

GEORGE: None at all.

LINTON: Well, this has me beaten.

GEORGE: Me too.

LINTON: Come on George, what you did the girl?

GEORGE: Nothing! You remember that afternoon I saw you
             here with Barten? She was supposed to meet me
             here that same evening.

LINTON: And she didn't?

GEORGE: No. Then out of the clear blue sky I hear she
             getting married to Samuels.

LINTON: Just like that?

GEORGE: Just like that.

LINTON: And what she said to you?

GEORGE: Nothing. I phoned her, sent messages, wrote to
             her, went to the house to see her...nothing doing.

LINTON: You must have done her something, George.

GEORGE: No, I tell you, man. And even if I did do her
             something, shouldn't she talk it over with me,
             instead of just taking off and marrying another
             man?

LINTON: You never could tell where you stand with those
             quiet women anyway.

GEORGE: She's a woman off my own heart, Linton. And it
             ain't going to end like this.

LINTON: What you going to do?

             [George does not answer]

             Well, there's still Irma.

GEORGE: Ah...! *[He gets up and starts pacing]*

LINTON: If you ask me, she has more going for her than
             Mildred.

GEORGE: *[With sarcasm]* She come from better family, eh?

LINTON: That's what's getting in your way?

GEORGE: Good family and no money. What use is that to
             me?

LINTON: Your problem is that you think money is every-
             thing. They mightn't have much money, but they
             have plenty connections. Don't underestimate
             the importance of connections.

GEORGE: *[Not wishing to continue the discussion. He stops
             pacing]* Ley me ask you something: When is
             Samuels leaving for Canada?

LINTON: In about two weeks. Why?

GEORGE: Mildred leaving with him?

LINTON: No. She has to wait for her papers from Immigra-
             tion.

GEORGE: You sure?

LINTON: Of course I'm...Now, wait a minute! Don't start
             thinking nonsense now.

GEORGE: She not moving from here, Linton. Between you
             and me, she not setting foot off this island.

LINTON: So you're going to stop her from going to her
             husband?

GEORGE: She had no call to marry him.

LINTON: Forget about the women, George.

GEORGE: Don't tell me what to do, man! *[Pause]* A mistake,
             Linton, a simple mistake that I goin' put right.

LINTON: Life is so shit-up it's a shame. Here you are refusing to give up on a woman who has willingly married another man. And there is Stanley, ready to give an arm and a leg to have Irma, who doesn't have eyes for anybody but you, who couldn't give a shit about whether she lives forever or falls down dead tonight!

GEORGE: Stanley Barten interested in Irma?

LINTON: You don't know that?

GEORGE: The son-of-a-bitch. *[Pause]*

LINTON: Why do you hate that man so?

GEORGE: Hate him? I don't hate him.

             [Irma bursts in. She seems to be very disturbed]

IRMA: Oh George! I've searched every place for you!

GEORGE: What happened? What's the matter?

             [She comes into his arms]

IRMA: Hold me, George, hold me tight. *[She rests her head against his shoulder and sobs bitterly]*

GEORGE: Okay, baby, relax it. There, tell me what happened now.

IRMA: It's, it's mother. We had a big quarrel.

GEORGE: Over what?

IRMA: You. *[She starts to cry again]*

GEORGE: *[Leading her towards a chair]* Okay, okay, don't worry about it. Sit down here and stop crying. That's it. I'll go get you some water. *[George leaves]*

LINTON: *[He looks at her speculatively]* All this isn't necessary, you know.

IRMA: *[Still half weeping]* What you say?

LINTON: I said, your little act isn't necessary.

IRMA: What act?

LINTON: Don't play games, Irma. You're too tough for your mother to upset you this much.

IRMA: Honest to God, we had a quarrel. She asked me to leave.

            [Phone is heard inside]

LINTON: Even if she did, you know she wasn't serious. You think George is stupid? He's going to see straight through you.

IRMA: Oh, shut up! He and I love each other, that's all.

LINTON: *[Sarcastically]* But you think you need to help things along a little bit, eh?

IRMA: Leave me alone and go mind your own business!

            [George enters with water and phone. She drinks]

GEORGE: Phone for you.

IRMA: Who is it?

GEORGE: They say is your mother.

IRMA: I don't want to talk to her.

GEORGE: Tell her.

IRMA: *[Grabbing the phone]* Hello, yes, it's me. No! I'm not coming home. Where I go is my business.

[She slams the phone down]

LINTON: Now all hell is going to break loose.

IRMA: Big deal!

GEORGE: What you think she'll do?

LINTON: The best thing is for Irma to go home before she does anything.

IRMA: I can't go home.

LINTON: Why not?

IRMA: She isn't going to throw me out and take me back in as she likes.

LINTON: For heaven's sake George, let her go home. If Mrs. Peebles comes here and sees you together, things could get nasty.

GEORGE: *[Decisively]* What the heck! If Irma wants to be with me, she wants to be with me.

LINTON: I need a brandy. *[He exits]*

IRMA: You're afraid there might be trouble? *[He doesn't answer]* Don't worry, darling, there isn't going to be any.

GEORGE: What exactly happened?

IRMA: Just as I told you. She heard we were in love and asked me to stop seeing you. Do you know what?

GEORGE: What?

IRMA: She wants me to marry Stanley Barten. Stanley Barten of all people!

GEORGE: So?

IRMA:	I told her she was crazy. That it's you I love. So, she got more annoyed and told me I was either going to obey her or leave. So I left.
GEORGE:	But couldn't you have gone to some of your other family until things cool off?
IRMA:	I did. I went to my uncle, but she called him up and then he started lecturing me too. *[Tears are creeping into her voice]* There's no place else I can go, George. No one else I can turn to but you.
GEORGE:	Okay, okay. Don't start upsetting yourself again. Things are going to work themselves out.

[Linton returns with a drink]

LINTON:	*[To George]* Would you like one?
GEORGE:	No, I'll manage.
LINTON:	*[To Irma]* Would you?
IRMA:	Yes, please. *[He is about to get her a drink when Sarah rushes in breathlessly]*
SARAH:	Miss Irma...you mother...she tek in bad...she sick bad, bad...
IRMA:	Go back home and tell her that if she thinks she's going to fool me with any of her acting tonight, she's crazy.
SARAH:	She sick bad for true, Miss Irma. Come go wid me to find de doctor.
IRMA:	Why don't you phone him?
SARAH:	I phone already but he not there. Faith to God, Miss Irma, she tek in bad in truth!
LINTON:	Can't you see it's no joke?

IRMA: If you're so concerned, why don't you go?

SARAH: Please, Mr. Gumbs. Please come wid me.

LINTON: *[Finishing his drink]* Let's go. *[They leave hurriedly]*

IRMA: Mother stops at nothing to have her own way.

GEORGE: Has it occurred to you that she might really be sick?

IRMA: It's just an act.

GEORGE: Sarah sounded pretty earnest to me.

IRMA: My mother is a good actress. She could fool Sarah but she can't fool me. Believe me, it's okay. I know my mother. *[She kisses him]* Let's get out of here.

GEORGE: And go where?

IRMA: How about your place?

GEORGE: Sounds good to me.

              [They leave. Lights fade out]

<u>SCENE VI</u>

[The Peebles' verandah a week later. Mildred is waiting for someone and is impatient. Presently she goes toward the house and calls urgently]

MILDRED: Sarah! Hurry up!

SARAH: *[From inside]* Wait no. Me coming right now.

MILDRED: Stop the coming and come.

              [She sits down again. In a short while she gets up and goes back towards the house]

Sarah! I going and leave you.

SARAH: *[Entering slightly annoyed]* You restless, eh? Me giving the house little air until they bring back Miss Jane from hospital. Wha' hurry you in?

MILDRED: I don't want her to come and meet me here.

SARAH: Just stay wey you be. She sick bad, so as she come me just bringing her out here for little air and then me putting she to bed and we could go 'bout we business. Go back go sit down.

MILDRED: But if she sick so bad who going look after her tonight?

SARAH: Not me. That not my concern. If she pan dying and she own daughter could be running wile all over the world, wha you say to me? As me put she in she bed that's it. Is gone me gone. *[Door bell rings inside]* That must be she they bring now. *[She exits]*

MILDRED: Hurry up!

[She goes back to sit down but curiosity gets the better of her so she creeps up to the door to peep inside]

SARAH: *[From inside]* Me ain't tired telling you when you ring the bell you must wait until I answer the door and don't just walk into the people house.

LINTON: Ah, come on, Sarah, you know I'm like one of the family.

SARAH: When Miss Jane here you could do what you like. When is me in charge you wait until I open the door.

LINTON: Ah, don't be so damn fussy.

SARAH: You hear what me say though.

[The voices get closer until Sarah re-enters]

SARAH: Is only Stanley Barten and Linton Gumbs. They always have to be in everything.

MILDRED: You see there now. Me going leave you.

SARAH: Is fraid you fraid them? Relax yourself.

LINTON: *[From inside]* Somebody out there with you, Sarah?

MILDRED: Look at this. I...

LINTON: *[Entering]* Oh, it's Mildred. I thought it might have been Irma.

STANLEY: *[From inside]* Did you say it was Irma?

LINTON: What are you doing here still? Aren't you supposed to be in Canada?

STANLEY: *[Entering with a bouquet of flowers]* Where is she?

LINTON: It isn't Irma. It's Mildred. *[To Mildred]* Come, sit down here and talk to me.
               [They sit]

STANLEY: *[To Sarah]* When is Irma coming back?

SARAH: It suppose to be tomorrow.

STANLEY: Does she know how sick her mother is?

SARAH: I don't know. I tell her but she ain't believe me.

STANLEY: How do you know she's coming tomorrow?

SARAH: She sent a cable.

STANLEY: She did? What did she say?

SARAH: Ley me go bring it so you could see for yourself.
            [She exits]

LINTON: So your papers are not fixed as yet?

MILDRED: No, not as yet.

LINTON: Did you come to welcome Mrs. Peebles home too?

MILDRED: No, not really.

LINTON: It's a sad case, isn't it?

MILDRED: Yes.

LINTON: You're as strong as an ox today; tomorrow, with-
            out warning you're like a baby again. *[With an
            effort to break off his thoughts]* Ah well, I suppose
            it's better than being dead.

SARAH: *[Returning with cable]* Look it here.

STANLEY: You'd better put these flowers in some water so
            they'll be fresh when Mrs. P gets home.

SARAH: *[Regarding him with disdain]* Alright. *[She exits]*

STANLEY: I say, Linton, listen to this cable from Irma. *[He
            reads to Linton]* "Mother, hope you're not still
            upset about my taking off so suddenly. Will be
            home Sunday with big surprise." What do you
            think that will be?

LINTON: What do you think?

STANLEY: I'd rather not think, Linton.

LINTON: Expect the worse.

STANLEY: I can't...I just can't believe she would run off with
            George O'Brien.

LINTON: Well, the evidence certainly points that way. I left
             them at the restaurant on Saturday night and on
             Sunday morning they had both checked out on
             the same flight for the same place.

STANLEY: There must be some other explanation.

LINTON: There's no doubt in mind they're together. Chances
             are they're even married by now.

STANLEY: No! I rather think your imagination is working
             overtime, Linton.

LINTON: It would not be as bad for you as you think, you
             know. As a matter of fact, it might well be a
             blessing in disguise.

IRMA: *[From inside]* Mother! Yoo, hoo! Mother!

STANLEY: It's Irma!

IRMA: *[Still from inside]* Maybe she's outside in her
             garden.

             [She enters and is surprised to see visitors]

             My goodness! How did you know we were coming
             home today? *[Calling back inside]* There's a whole
             welcoming party out here, darling. Come and join
             it. Did mother phone the airlines and found out
             we couldn't get a flight for tomorrow?

STANLEY: Irma!

             [George enters]

IRMA: *[Kissing Stanley on his cheek]* It's not the end of the
             world, Stan. We'll always be good friends.

             *[George and Mildred stare intensely at each other.
             She drops her gaze but not before Irma notices the
             silent communication. She goes over to Mildred
             and holds out the ring for her to see]* Like it?

MILDRED: It…it's b-beautiful.

IRMA: But do you like it?

MILDRED: Y-yes.

IRMA: We got married in Antigua and then we flew to
             Nevis for our honeymoon. It was heavenly. We had
             such a gorgeous time I didn't want to leave. But we
             had to hurry back. You know my husband and his
             precious hotel.

             *[Unable to contain herself anymore, Mildred breaks
             down and sobs]*

             She's crying! Look at that, darling, isn't it nice?
             She's so happy for us she's crying!

             [George stares at Irma. Murder is in his eyes]

LINTON: Irma! Irma!, there's something you ought to know.

IRMA: Oh, no! Not another one of your lectures, please.
             I'm in too good a mood. Save it until I'm depressed
             so you can liven me up.

LINTON: I'm not about to lecture you. I only want to tell you
             about your mother.

IRMA: Well, that's exactly what I'm waiting to hear.
             Where is she?

LINTON: *[Trying to break the news as gently as possible]* It's
             like this, Irma…

             *[As he is speaking, Sarah pushes Mrs. P. onto the
             verandah in a wheel chair. Nobody notices for a
             while]*

             …Your mother was not exppcting you today.
             Neither were we. Actually, we're here to welcome
             her home, not you.

IRMA: *[She's suddenly aware that all is not well]* What do
               you mean?

LINTON: She had a stroke. I don't want you to take this
               badly...but...

               *[By now all eyes are fixed on the pitiful sight of Mrs.
               Peebles. A broken, shrunken, feeble old lady in a
               wheel chair. Irma is the last to become aware of her
               presence. For a moment nothing is said]*

IRMA: *[Chocked with emotions and disbelief]* M-mother?
               [Then with unequalled anguished] Mother! Oh
               God! Oh God! Noooo!

               *[She hurls herself at her mother's feet crying bit-
               terly. All lights fade out leaving a single spotlight on
               mother and daughter which slowly fades out as
               well.]*

ACT TWO

<u>SCENE I</u>

Nine months later. The set remains the same as Act I except for the area which housed the restaurant. This has now become Mildred's bedroom.

It is just after sunset. As the lights come up, Mrs. P. is seen on the verandah sitting in her wheel chair knitting. George and Irma have just returned from the cocktail party and opening ceremony of the hotel he was building. Linton, who also attended the party, has dropped by to say hello to Mrs. Peebles. We hear them talking inside.

IRMA: My goodness! What a party that was!

LINTON: I've got a hand it to you, George, you couldn't have done a finer job on that hotel. The workmanship is superb.

GEORGE: Naturally.

IRMA: All those people! The whole island must have been at the opening. I'm so sorry Mother wasn't there. Sarah! Mother! Where's everybody? *[Entering]* Ah! Here she is! I might have known I'd find you here.

GEORGE: Go on out, Linton. I'll hang up my jacket and bring you a brandy.

IRMA: Oh, Mother the party was lovely.

[Linton enters]

LINTON: Hello Mrs. P. How are you keeping?

MRS. P.   *[Still weak but much recovered since we saw her last]* So so, Linton, coming along slowly.

LINTON: You're not coming along slowly at all. You're doing wonders.

MRS. P.   Well, God is good.

IRMA: Everybody asked for you, Mother. Even the Governor.

MRS. P.   *[Pleased]* He did?

IRMA: And the Chief Minister too. Says he has to drop by to see you soon.

MRS. P.   Well, it's nice to know I'm not forgotten. If everybody was only like you, Linton...you never gave me up.

LINTON: Not only me. You still have lots of friends.

MRS. P.   Oh, it's not like it used to be. Nobody has any use for a crippled old lady.

IRMA: You know we should throw a party like we used to.

MRS. P: My time for that is passed.

             [George enters]

IRMA: Really, let's do. We could invite the Chief Minister and the Governor and everybody. *[To George]* What do you think, darling?

GEORGE: About what?

IRMA: Having a party?

GEORGE: When we do have a party, let's have it just for our
             friends, okay?

IRMA: We could invite everybody. It would be like old
             times. You'd have a great time, Mother. It's just
             what you need.

MRS. P: It could be. *[Then shaking her head]* No, my days
             for parties are over.

IRMA: Oh, Mother, you know how I hate to hear you say
             things like that. You'll soon be up and about, just
             as you always were.

MRS. P: *[Ignoring her]* Isn't my garden growing well, Linton?

LINTON: It's beautiful.

MRS. P: Sarah does her best with it, but it's nothing like
             when I was up and around.

LINTON: As the old saying goes: The hand of the master
             fatteneth the cattle.

MRS. P: Oh, Linton, you always say things to cheer me up.
             Well, I'd better get out of this draught before I
             catch a cold. *[She starts to wheel herself off]*

IRMA: Sarah!

MRS. P: No, don't call her. I'll manage by myself. *[She exits]*

LINTON: It's really nice of you to live here and look after her,
             Irma.

IRMA: It's the least I can do. George is who you should
             compliment. I never thought I'd be able to con-
             vince him to live here, but he did it just for me. It's
             not at all that bad, darling, is it?

GEORGE: You ever hear me complaining?

IRMA: Don't be so grouchy, dear.

GEORGE: *[Turning his attention to Linton]* So, you didn't think I'd be able to do it then?

LINTON: I must confess, I didn't expect you finish the hotel so soon.

GEORGE: The sooner you finish, the more money you make. Although the double shifts cost me more than I'd budgeted for.

LINTON: Did you make what you said you would?

GEORGE: Nearly, but not quite. Fell short by a few thousand dollars.

LINTON: Man, that's remarkable. Let's see now, it means you must have made a clear profit of over fifty thousand dollars. Not bad. Not exactly what you would call peanut change.

GEORGE: Ah, that's only the beginning. It's time now to move on to bigger and better things, like the hospital for example.

IRMA: I can't get over how many people were at the opening. And they were all so delighted with the hotel. Oh, darling, I'm so proud of you! *[She kisses him on his cheek]*

GEORGE: Why don't you get Linton another brandy and some lemonade for me too.

IRMA: You want a drink, Linton?

GEORGE: Linton always wants a drink.

IRMA: Sarah! Sarah! Why the devil doesn't she answer?

GEORGE: For heaven's sake do something for yourself for a change!

IRMA: What do you think I'm paying her for?

[George ignores her. She stares at him for a moment. She's annoyed but decides to go for the drink. Before she exits she swings around again]

I'm your wife you know, George, not your servant!

GEORGE: Just go get the damn...!

[She has left. He mutters under his breath]

Stupid bitch! As I was saying...What's the position with the hospital?

LINTON: I told you it's no problem. When the time comes I'll see to it you get the contract.

GEORGE: Look, since you mentioned it to me, I've been working on some designs. That's the deal I'm interested in: Designing the hospital...and, of course, building it as well.

LINTON: Well, building the hospital is one thing, but...designing it is a different matter altogether.

GEORGE: You could talk the Government into it.

LINTON: The problem is not so much with Government. Britain is putting up most of the money. She mightn't go for it.

GEORGE: There must be something you could do.

LINTON: I'll tell you what. When you finish the drawings, give me a copy . I can't promise anything, but I'll look into it.

GEORGE: I expect you to give it your best shot, Linton.

LINTON: I'll give it my best shot. That you can depend on

GEORGE: Alright. You'll have a copy as soon as I'm finished. By the way, I hear your friend isn't doing too well with his estate.

LINTON: Stanley? Hitting the bottle too hard, that's what's wrong.

GEORGE: You think he'd be willing to sell some of that land?

LINTON: I doubt it. You want to buy land?

GEORGE: You never know.

LINTON: I don't think he'd sell.

GEORGE: Why not? He doesn't know what to do with it. Look at all the land he has sitting down not making any money.

LINTON: I agree with you. What he should do is go into real estate.

GEORGE: He doesn't even have to do that. With the price of food these days, if he knows what he's doing, he could make a fortune.

LINTON: I'm not so sure about that.

GEORGE: Let me get my hand on some of that land and you'll see. You telling me a farm supplying vegetables, milk and eggs to the whole island can't make money?

LINTON: Well, you could probably squeeze money out of stone, George, but with Stanley it's a different matter. Anyway, if you planning to buy land you might as well start looking elsewhere. Normally he doesn't want to sell. You, he wouldn't sell a tass to save his life.

[Irma enters with drinks]

GEORGE: Oh, I know that. Don't worry yourself. I know that.

IRMA: Here you are, Linton. Here you are, sir. Well, Linton, how does a party sound to you?

LINTON: Not bad. I'm always in the mood for a party.

IRMA: It would be good for Mother. She would see all her friends again. And for you too, dear. He works so hard.

LINTON: It agrees with him.

IRMA: But he needs to rest. To relax. *[To George];* Now you've finished the hotel and made so much money we should go away for a little holiday.

GEORGE: I'm building two houses, remember?

IRMA: Sure, I remember. I got you one of the contracts, didn't I? But we're not going to be gone forever.

GEORGE: What contract you got me?

IRMA: You know the...Ah! never mind. A holiday will do us both a lot of good, George.

GEORGE: There's no way I can go any place now, Irma. There're those two houses, plus I have to go and see a client about a third one in a short while.

IRMA: Tonight! You see what I mean Linton, he doesn't give himself any peace. Please, George, think about it. After the party we...

GEORGE: And didn't you hear your mother saying she doesn't want any party?

IRMA: But she does want a party.

GEORGE: I distinctly heard her saying...

IRMA: I know she does, darling!

GEORGE: Oh, I forgot…I keep forgetting how well you know
            your mother.

IRMA: Please! *[Pause]* When are you going to stop accus-
            ing me?

LINTON: Look, I'd better be leaving now.

GEORGE: Wait for me. I'm leaving now myself.

LINTON: Take care of yourself, Irma.

            [Linton goes towards the house]

GEORGE: Forgetting your way around? You can still get to
            the garage through here.

            [He points to an exit]

LINTON: No, no. I'm going to say so long to Mrs. P.

GEORGE: Well, I'll get those drawings to you soon.

LINTON: Will do.

            [He exits. George is also on his way out]

IRMA: George?

GEORGE: What is it now?

IRMA: You're coming back soon?

GEORGE: Maybe, maybe not.

IRMA: Try and come back soon.

GEORGE: Don't wait up for me.

IRMA: I'm going to wait right here for you. So come back
            now, okay?

            [He shrugs his shoulders and leaves]

I'm serious, George. I'll be right here when you get
back.

*[She settles down for the long wait. Presently
Sarah enters]*

SARAH: Stanley here to you.

IRMA: *[Under her breath]* What the hell does he want
now? *[To Sarah]* Why is it that every time I call you,
you're never around?

SARAH: *[Innocently]* But I always aroun'.

IRMA: So you hear me calling and not answering me
then?

SARAH: Me never hear you call and don't answer you.

IRMA: Don't talk back to me like that!

SARAH: You ask me a question an' me answer you.

IRMA: Now wait a minute. Who died and left you a
fortune?

SARAH: Lord have mercy, eh! You mother waiting pan me.

IRMA: Keep it up. You just keep up this attitude and
when I start to deal with you, run to Mother and
see how that will help you!

[Sarah exits grumbling under her breath]

SARAH: Me no know wha' wrong wid you, you know, but
me no 'fraid you.

IRMA: Sarah! Come ba...

[Stanley enters]

STANLEY: Irma!

IRMA: Hello, Stanley.

STANLEY: Irma, may I have a word with you?

IRMA: Sure, sit down.

STANLEY: Where's O'Brien?

IRMA: He's gone to see a client.

STANLEY: Is that what he told you?

IRMA: Why?

STANLEY: Look, Irma, I don't want to offend you, or any such thing...How do I say this? It's like this...

IRMA: Before you go any further, Stanley, let me reassure you: George and I have been happily married for nine months now and nothing is going to change that.

STANLEY: Sometimes, you make it so painful to talk to you.

IRMA: I'm sick and tired of you forever trying to get me to turn my back on him. Just accept things the way they are.

STANLEY: I've come to grips with the fact that I've lost you, Irma. Believe me, I have.

IRMA: Okay, so what were you saying then?

STANLEY: It's difficult for me to say it...George is carrying on an affair with Mildred Sweeney.

IRMA: Impossible. Telling me lies isn't going to help.

STANLEY: *[Explosively]* What do you think I am, Irma? Yes! My feelings for you are strong. It's not a thing I can stop overnight. But I would never lie to you.

IRMA:	*[Sarcastically]* How noble. Let me put it this way then: I know it can't be true, and nothing you say will make me believe you.
STANLEY:	You may not believe me, but that doesn't mean it isn't true.
IRMA:	Besides, Mildred is a simple Christian girl. She wouldn't risk such a scandal.
STANLEY:	Please, don't be so naive.
IRMA:	Look who's talking about being naive. She'll never get the chance. The church and her mother are watching her too closely.
STANLEY:	They meet secretly at her husband's house.
IRMA:	She doesn't have the guts to do it.
STANLEY:	But what about George?
IRMA:	He'll never do such a thing to me.
STANLEY:	Come with me, Irma. I'm sure they're meeting there tonight. You'll see for yourself.
IRMA:	You're just wasting your time, Stanley…and mine as well.
STANLEY:	Are you afraid it might be true?
IRMA:	Look, nothing is going to come between me and George. Not Mildred, not you, not anybody.
STANLEY:	Well, come and see then.
IRMA:	Will you stop annoying me!
STANLEY:	Don't let him make a fool of you, Irma.

IRMA: Let me tell you something, Stanley: Don't ever come back to me with a story like this about my husband.

STANLEY: Listen, Irma...

IRMA: And that's all I have to say about the matter. I don't want to hear anything else!

STANLEY: Okay, okay. *[Pause]* Understand one thing, Irma. It's only because of you...

IRMA: *[With annoyance]* Yes! I know, I know!

STANLEY: *[There is a long pause during which he hangs his head]* Good night. *[He walks away stiffly with as much dignity as the occasion will allow and leaves via the exit leading to the garage. Irma sits alone, becoming increasingly restless. She gets up and paces with uncertainty for a while. Then walks decisively towards the door to the house]*

IRMA: Sarah! Sarah!

SARAH: *[From inside]* Yes.

IRMA: Bring me a sweater.

               [Sarah brings the sweater and gives it to her silently. She puts it on. A certain determination is reflected in all her movements. The same determination is there as she walks off leaving through the exit that both George and Stanley used before. Sarah stands watching her go as the lights fade]

<u>SCENE II</u>

[Mildred's bedroom. As the lights go up Mildred is waiting for someone who is late. Rather than annoyed, she is nervous. There is a noise off stage (not necessarily heard by the audience). She is startled and calls out nervously]

MILDRED:	George, is that you? George?

GEORGE:	*[Off stage]* Yes, it's me. *[He enters]*

MILDRED:	*[Relieved]*Oh, I thought you weren't coming again. I was getting worried.

GEORGE:	*[Kissing her lightly]* Nothing to worry about. You know if I tell you I'll be here, I'll be here.

MILDRED:	It's just that whenever you're late I feel something has happened.

GEORGE:	I'm tired telling you you worry too much. Nothing is going to happen.

MILDRED:	That's easy for you to say.

GEORGE:	What you expect to happen? I got held up after the cocktail party, that's all.

MILDRED:	Was the party good?

GEORGE:	Pretty good. Good for business at least. A few people approached me about building houses for them.

MILDRED:	*[With admiration]* More houses again?

GEORGE:	*[With pride]*Well, you don't just build three or four and stop there, you know. There's lots of bread to be made, lots of ground to cover. *[With accusation]* You should be covering it with me.

MILDRED:	*[Sadly]* Well…it's too late now.

GEORGE:	It's never too late. You want it to be too late.

MILDRED:	If that was true, you think I'd run the risk to meet you here like this? And that's another thing, George: if we continue like this people are bound to find out.

GEORGE: *[He attempts to take her in his arms]* Come on.
              Don't start with that again.

MILDRED: It's not right, George. It's just not right.

GEORGE: Mildred, you realize how often we go through this
              same routine?

MILDRED: Why don't my papers come so I could go away in
              peace?

GEORGE: *[Annoyed]* Sometimes you make it sound as if it
              would be the end of the world if anyone finds out
              we're seeing each other.

MILDRED: But that's what it would be for me, George. Mama
              would kill me. I wouldn't be able to show my face
              any place.

GEORGE: *[Attempting to take her in his arms again]*Come on,
              quit worrying.

MILDRED: *[Resisting slightly]* It's not right, George. It's just
              not right.

GEORGE: We love each other, Mildred. That's all it takes to
              make it right. *[He kisses briefly, she pulls away]*

MILDRED: Oh George, think of me for once...

GEORGE: Think of you for once! Why the hell you don't try
              thinking of me for a change?

MILDRED: Please, George...

GEORGE: Don't please me, man! You have any idea what it's
              like to wake up one morning and the first thing
              you hear is that the woman you love is getting
              married to another man! You ever think about
              that?

MILDRED: You think it was any easier for me? You think it's
              any easier for me now?

GEORGE: You had no right to let it happen in the first place.

MILDRED: I couldn't help it, George. I told you that already. Sarah had warned me that the two of you had something going. And I was willing to die before I would believe it. And then…I came to the restaurant as we had planned…

GEORGE: You came to the restaurant? How come you never told me that before?

MILDRED: And then…and then, she was there in your lap hugging you up…and kissing you.

GEORGE: Wha…!

MILDRED: And…I couldn't take it, George, I just couldn't take it. Up to now I don't know how I got home that night, but I cried for days. Mother made all the wedding plans and the next thing I know…*[She cries]*

GEORGE: Five minutes earlier or five minutes later and everything would be different today.

MILDRED: What you say?

GEORGE: Nothing. Well, no point crying over split milk. And no point wallowing in it either.

MILDRED: What you mean?

GEORGE: We have to stop this hiding and seeking, Mildred. *[He takes her in his arms]* Time for us to stop behaving like two thieves.

MILDRED: It's not right, George…It's just not right.

            [This time she doesn't pull away. Lights fade out]

SCENE III

*[Later the same night. The Peebles' house. Moon light. Irma
enters from the garage followed by Stanley]*

IRMA: Go home and leave me alone, Stanley! You've
               spied on me enough for one night!

STANLEY: I told you, Irma. I wasn't spying on you.

IRMA: What you call it then?

STANLEY: After I left you this evening I was upset. I couldn't
               go home that way. So I was standing at the corner
               debating whether or not I should come back and
               try to make it up with you. When I saw you leaving
               I guessed where you were going. I couldn't let you
               go through it alone, Irma.

IRMA: Well, if you're offering a shoulder for me to cry on,
               I don't need one.

STANLEY: Why do you detest me so much?

IRMA: Go on. Laugh your head off.

STANLEY: You know I will never laugh at you, Irma.

IRMA: *[Collapsing in his arms as if a great burden has
               suddenly become too much to bear]* Oh,
               Stanley!...*[She cries. He comforts her in silence
               allowing the tears to ease the pain]* Take me away,
               Stanley. Take me away. *[Pause]*

STANLEY: It's something I've always dreamt of doing, Irma.

IRMA: You don't have to dream anymore.

STANLEY: But...but not at a time like this.

IRMA: *[Scornfully]* Oh, you and your Victorian ideals.

STANLEY: What's wrong with wanting our love to be pure and beautiful, instead of...an act of revenge?

IRMA: *[Absent-mindedly]* Revenge.

STANLEY: Confront him with it when he comes, Irma. File for divorce. After that you and I...

IRMA: Can live happily ever after? No. There're too many things to be done before that.

STANLEY: Such as?

IRMA: Would you help me if I told you?

STANLEY: Do you have to ask?

IRMA: Why hasn't she gone to her husband?

STANLEY: I understand her papers are not fixed as yet.

IRMA: That's a lie. She must have got them by now. She doesn't intend to leave.

STANLEY: Or maybe he's preventing her. He might have managed to get his hands on the papers and wouldn't let her have them. You know how conniving...

IRMA: Never mind what it is! Can you contact the Canadian Embassy and have her papers fixed?

STANLEY: It...it would be difficult.

IRMA: But you can do it?

STANLEY: It's not that I don't want...

IRMA: Why would it be difficult? The High Commissioner and your father were good friends.

STANLEY: But I haven't seen him in ages. We're out of touch.

IRMA: All you have to do, Stanley, is go and see him personally.

STANLEY: But he might not remember me.

IRMA: *[Impatiently]* Oh for heaven's sake! Tell him who you are. Take him a case of rum as a gift and tell him you're Mr. Barten's son. He'll be happy to do you a small favor. *[Pause]* Will you try it for me!

STANLEY: I suppose I can. Yes.

IRMA: Well, look after that for me, Stanley. And as soon as you have the papers, book her on the first flight to Canada. I'll handle the rest myself.

STANLEY: But I don't see what good this is going to do, Irma.

IRMA: Just trust me, okay? *[He doesn't respond]* The air must be clean before love can be pure and beautiful, darling. *[She kisses him lightly]* But you'd better be going now. George might come back soon.

STANLEY: Good. We can tell him about the divorce and have it over and done with.

IRMA: No, no! I'll tell him when the time is right. Just look after that matter for me as soon as possible.

STANLEY: Are you going to confront him?

IRMA: When the time is right, darling.

STANLEY: Okay, I'll start working on it immediately.

IRMA: Do that. *[He leaves]* I can't wait to move that bitch out of my way. *[She sits, all wrapped up in her plans. George enters. He is spot-lighted while the lights on Irma fade. On his way in he pauses]*

GEORGE: Who is it?

IRMA: *[From the darkness]* Will you shut your mouth and mind you wake mother! *[She approaches him]*

GEORGE: What the...!

IRMA: Have you no consideration for me, George? You kept me waiting here all night.

GEORGE: I told you I was going to be late.

IRMA: But I told you I would wait for you.

GEORGE: Why didn't you go to bed after you didn't see me?

IRMA: *[Almost screaming at him]* I told you George. I told you I was going to wait for you!

GEORGE: Who's waking your mother now?

IRMA: Where are you coming from?

GEORGE: Now wait a minute. Since when I don't have the right to come and go as I like in my own house?

IRMA: I asked you a simple question...Where are you coming from?

MRS. P: *[From inside]* Irma, is anything wrong?

IRMA: Nothing is wrong, mother. What are you doing out of bed at this time? Go back to sleep. Answer me, George.

GEORGE: Let me ask you something. What argument you holding with me at this hour of night?

IRMA: That is the whole trouble. Every time I open my mouth to discuss something with you, you say I'm arguing! What is going to become of us if we can't sit down and talk? And we have a lot to talk about. A hell of a lot.

GEORGE: Well, I never see! Let me remind you, Irma. I live under my own roof...

IRMA: George! I am your wife! We both live together.

GEORGE: And the moment you don't like the hour I come home at night, or anything else I do for that matter, just let me know. I'd be happy to find some place else for you and your mother to live.

IRMA: No, George, no. You may be paying the mortgage on this house, you may have all the money in the world, but you're never going to make a fool of me.

GEORGE: I done say what I have to say. *[He exits]*

IRMA: As powerful as you think you are, you're never going to walk on me.

MRS. P: *[Entering in wheel chair]* Irma, shouldn't you be in bed, child?

IRMA: What are you coming out here for, Mother? Go ahead back to sleep. *[Mrs. P. does not respond but sits staring at her]* Don't look at me like that!

MRS. P: Another quarrel again.

IRMA: It was not a quarrel. Would you keep out of it!

MRS. P: Well, I'm too old now to worry. You make your bed, you lie on it.

IRMA: I told you, don't look at me like that! *[Pause]* Mildred Sweeney! She's the cause of all our troubles. But not anymore. I'm going to send her packing to her husband. Then George and I will be happy. And you too, Mother.

MRS. P: Come, it's very late. Let's go to sleep.

            [Lights fade as they exit]

SCENE IV

[Mid-afternoon. George and Linton are sitting on the verandah]

GEORGE: What's the exact position with the hospital, man? You say the Government likes the designs?

LINTON: Government is not the problem, I told you. England doesn't like the idea.

GEORGE: Why? Because I'm not a qualified Architect?

LINTON: That might be part of the problem. But I think I could get around it. Just leave things to me at the moment, okay? Go ahead telling me about the farm.

GEORGE: Look, tell them that if they agree to use my designs, I will build the hospital at cost price. The profits and part of my salary will become my donation to the building.

LINTON: Seriously?

GEORGE: You ever know me to bullshit about things like that?

LINTON: That will make a hell of a difference.

GEORGE: I figured it would.

LINTON: It certainly would. I don't think we'll have any trouble getting them to agree to that.

GEORGE: Listen, let's put the proposal to the Chief Minister now.

LINTON: Now?

GEORGE: Why not?

LINTON: What's the hurry?

GEORGE: Now is as good a time as any.

LINTON: Well, it's no point going now, anyway. He's at some school concert and wouldn't be back until to-night.

GEORGE: So we'll go tonight then?

LINTON: Okay. If that's what you want, we'll go and see him tonight. Go on telling me about the farm.

GEORGE: Nothing to tell, really. I'm about to close a deal on some of the finest land on the island, that's all.

LINTON: You actually got some land to buy?

GEORGE: You know I don't make joke.

LINTON: How come I haven't heard anything about it?

GEORGE: That's the beauty of it. It's too hard for a local man to buy good land in this place, so I became a Canadian Company and fooled everybody.

LINTON: What the hell are you talking about?

GEORGE: It's like this: I've been posing as a foreign company and letting my lawyers do all the negotiations for me. It cost me a pretty penny, but I couldn't buy it myself if I was going to pay twice as much. *[He smiles devilishly and we get the impression that somehow he is mocking Linton]* Not bad for a poor boy with no education, eh?

LINTON: Sounds interesting. Where about is this land?

GEORGE: You wouldn't believe.

LINTON: Try me.

GEORGE: I'll do better than that. *[Getting up]* Come, I'll show it to you before we go see the Minister.

LINTON: *[Getting up too]* Okay. *[They start moving off. George stops suddenly and cuffs his palm]*

GEORGE: Oh, no!

LINTON: Forgot to do something?

GEORGE: Yea. I have an appointment tonight. Sarah! Sarah!

LINTON: Business?

GEORGE: No. Nothing serious. It could wait until later. *[He pulls out a note book and a pen and starts writing a note]*

SARAH: *[Entering from the house]* You call me, sah?

GEORGE: *[Pulling her aside]* Carry this note and give it to Mildred for me. *[To Linton]* Come, we go. *[Linton exits. George turns back to Sarah]* Make haste and carry it now, you know. *[He exits. Sarah is trying to put the note in her bosom as Irma enters from house]*

IRMA: What did he give you?

SARAH: Nothing ma'am.

IRMA: Don't play the fool with me Sarah.

SARAH: For true, for true, is nothing.

IRMA: Listen to me: Mother might want you around here and George might be harboring you as well, but you know me better than that. And I'm warning you, Sarah, don't play the fool with me.

SARAH: *[Coming sullenly to Irma and giving her the note]* Ley me no put meself in people business see.

IRMA: *[Pulling the note from her]* Now go back inside and finish what you were doing. *[As Sarah exits she reads the note]*

SARAH: Me warn Mildred and warn Mildred 'till me tired.

    [She exits]

IRMA: *[Irma goes to the phone and dials]* Hello, Stanley? Did you get those papers fixed for me? Good, and did you get the flight booked? Good. How soon? In a week. Okay, that's good enough. Have the papers ready. I'm coming to get them now. No, not as yet. I'll speak to him about the divorce when the time is right.

    [Lights fade out]

SCENE V

[Mildred's bedroom. As the lights go up, we see Mildred in much the same nervous condition as she was in Scene II. Again she is startled by a noise off stage and calls out]

MILDRED: George? Is that you George? *[Irma enters and stands looking at Mildred. She says quietly]*

IRMA: George will not be coming back here.

MILDRED: It's, it's not...he was not coming here for...

IRMA: Never mind what he was coming for. I'm here in his place, so we could have a nice heart to heart talk.

MILDRED: A-about what? *[She looks nervously towards the entrance]*

IRMA: There's nothing to be afraid of. I came here alone and I'm not going to hurt you. *[Unable to meet her gaze, Mildred stares at the floor]* Why haven't you gone to your husband?

MILDRED: My papers, I never got them.

IRMA: Why didn't you check with the Embassy?

MILDRED: I did.

IRMA: And?

MILDRED: They say they sent them. But I never got them.

IRMA: Is that all that's keeping you from going to your...

MILDRED: Y-yes.

IRMA: Well, I'll tell you what. I've gone through a lot of trouble to have those papers fixed for you. *[She gives the papers to her]* If you really wanted them you could have had them fixed yourself. But, that's beside the point. I've also booked you on a flight for Canada which leaves in a week. Do you have enough money to pay for the ticket? *[Mildred shakes her head]* Then, phone your husband and let him cable you the money. *[Pause]* Will he do it? *[Mildred nods her head]* Well, will he?

MILDRED: Yes.

IRMA   So, you have a long week to get your stuff together and then you're on your way. Enjoy your flight. *[She stares moving off. Before she exits she turns back]* Just one more thing: You must tell my husband nothing of this. You hear me? *[Mildred nods her head]* Because if he stops you from going...if for any reason under the sun you're still on this island after next week, God have mercy on you. *[She exits. The lights fade leaving just a spot light on Mildred. She buries her head in her lap and cries bitterly]*

SCENE VI

[George is sitting on the verandah by himself. Linton enters]

LINTON: Hey man! What you doing out there all by your-
            self?

GEORGE: Just taking life easy.

LINTON: *[Joining him]* What's the matter with you now? The
            woman giving trouble again?

GEORGE: What woman?

LINTON: The same one.

GEORGE: I don't know what you're talking about.

LINTON: You don't intend to let the girl go to her husband,
            eh?

GEORGE: *[Getting a bit annoyed]* Look, that's what you come
            all the way out here to ask me?

LINTON: What are you getting so hot about?

GEORGE: Who's getting hot?

LINTON: *[Allowing the matter to rest]* Actually, I've come to
            ask you a favor.

GEORGE: *[With sarcasm]* Since when is the prospering
            Permanent Secretary asking favors of a poor man
            like me? Did you speak to the Chief Minister?

LINTON: Yeah, but things are still pretty much the same.

GEORGE: England still giving trouble?

LINTON: You might say that. But don't worry, we're work-
            ing hard on it. The Minister and I are going to
            London to talk...

GEORGE: Talk, talk, talk! When am I going to see some action, man.

LINTON: We're doing all we can, George. The British Government is holding up the works.

GEORGE: When are you guys going to stop dancing to whatever tune Britain plays?

LINTON: Come on, George, we're still a colony, what you expect us to do?

GEORGE: Stop being a colony.

LINTON: Look, we're doing our best and you know it! After all, Britain is putting up three-quarters of the money. There's not very much we can tell them.

GEORGE: Then get the money from some place else! Canada...

LINTON: What difference is that going to make? Canada will probably not only demand that she uses her own architects and contractors, but may even stipulate that all building materials be bought from her even though we may be able to get them cheaper elsewhere. And if you don't look sharp, she might even want to send down her own workmen and all.

GEORGE: All these are matters which can be dealt with in negotiating the loan. The point is, has any effort been made to get the money elsewhere?

LINTON: Take it from me, George, we're doing the absolute best that can be done. To be quite honest with you, Britain has all but said that if her architects aren't used, she isn't going to come up with the money. I'm telling you, I had to go through hell itself just to get them to agree to let you build...

GEORGE: Building the hospital is not enough.

LINTON: For heaven's sake, George! It's true you're not
            going to make as much money...

GEORGE: To hell with the money! I have already made it
            clear that if my design is used I will build the
            hospital at cost price. Money has nothing to do
            with it.

LINTON: You may not need the money, George, but what
            about me? I have commitments, you know. And I
            have already worked double time, to swing this
            job your way. If you were satisfied with building
            the hospital it would have been almost finished by
            now; and we would both be making money.

GEORGE: There is not a time you have worked for me that
            I have not paid you and paid you very well.

LINTON: I do not work for you. You scratch my back and I
            scratch yours.

GEORGE: Get me the hospital, Linton. Get me the hospital
            and you may never need to have your back
            scratched again.

LINTON: I tell you I'm doing the best I can. Why are you so
            damn obsessed with this hospital? *[Pause]*

GEORGE: You wouldn't understand, Linton. *[Pause]* It has
            to do with achievement, posterity, if you wish to
            call it that. True, I designed and built some of the
            finest houses on this island, but a hospital is
            different. It's a monument. You understand what
            I'm saying?

LINTON: Sure, sure I understand.

GEORGE: No, Linton, you haven't got a clue.

LINTON: You're sitting pretty, George. You could afford to dream. I have to look about the very practical business of making two ends meet from day to day.

GEORGE: *[He gives off a sigh which indicates the matter is dismissed]* What favor you wanted to ask me?

LINTON: Maybe now is not a good time.

GEORGE: Up to you.

LINTON: It concerns Stanley.

GEORGE: What about him?

LINTON: The man is literally going to pieces.

GEORGE: Would you like me to send a carpenter over to patch him up?

LINTON: He is in a serious state of affairs, George. He's at the point of a nervous breakdown.

GEORGE: What the hell does that have to do with me? I'm a builder you know, not a psychiatrist.

LINTON: All I'm asking is that you give him a break, George. Give him a chance to finish harvesting the crop on the land you bought from him.

GEORGE: The crop is mine. I bought it. Why should I let him harvest it?

LINTON: He says the crop wasn't included in the price.

GEORGE: I bought the land. As far as I'm concerned the crop was included in the price. And if he doesn't agree, he could get his lawyer.

LINTON: It is clearly an oversight. If the price of the crop was included, you know it would have cost you much, much more.

GEORGE: The land is mine, along with everything in it and
            on it. And you should advise him not to so much
            as set foot on it.

LINTON: Have a heart, George. It's not the first time
            something like this has happened. Anybody else
            would let him harvest that crop.

GEORGE: I'm not anybody else. Business is business. I don't
            have any fancy degree, but you don't see me
            selling land to somebody and then turning around
            and expecting to harvest a crop from that same
            land.

LINTON: When he sold the land he had already started to
            harvest. His equipment...

GEORGE: It doesn't make any difference. The crop is still
            mine. If he want to buy it back from me, well,
            that's a different matter.

LINTON: It's not such a cut and dry issue, you know.

GEORGE: Well, if he thinks he has a case, let him take me
            to court and we could battle it out from there.
            That's all. Did he send you to ask me to ease him
            up?

LINTON: Sort of. He's taking it pretty badly.

GEORGE: Tell him to come and talk to me himself.

LINTON: You know he's not going to do that.

GEORGE: He too high and mighty to talk to me, eh?

LINTON: Jesus Christ, George. You've beaten the man on
            all fronts. What you want him to do now? Fall
            down on his face before you?

GEORGE: Why not? The first lesson poor people must learn
            is how to be humble.

LINTON: *[Shaking his head]* You're a hard man, you know.

GEORGE: I'm a hard man? I refuse to let people push their finger in my eye and I'm a hard man?

LINTON: Life is so shit up it's a shame. Look, let's forget it. Come we go down to the club. I'll buy you one.

GEORGE: Not tonight.

LINTON: You going to see the girl, eh?

GEORGE: You believe all I have to think 'bout is woman.

LINTON: Once upon a time you wouldn't be keeping me in the dark like this, you know.

GEORGE: Once upon a time you would have had that hospital job nailed down for me a long time ago.

LINTON: Don't worry about the hospital. You have to learn to let things ride. Sure you don't want to fire one?

GEORGE: Quite sure.

LINTON: Well, it's about time I had my first one for the evening. So, I'll just pop inside and say hi to Mrs. P. and then take off. *[He starts to leave]* And don't worry about the hospital. I have things under control. *[He exits]*

GEORGE: *[To himself]* Sure, sure.

             [Lights fade]

SCENE VII

[Mildred's bedroom. Dawn. George, in underwear only, is getting dressed. Mildred is lying in bed, propped up on her elbow, watching him]

GEORGE: What's on your mind?

MILDRED: Nothing.

GEORGE: How could it be nothing?

MILDRED: Nothing in particular. Just thinking how nice last
            night was.

GEORGE: Are you sure nothing is wrong?

MILDRED: Why you keep asking me that?

GEORGE: It's just not like you to say things like that.

MILDRED: Nothing is wrong, George. *[Pause]* You didn't
            enjoy last night?

GEORGE: Sure I enjoyed it...But it was different.

MILDRED: Maybe...maybe it's because I've stopped trying to
            fight what's between us.

GEORGE: I hope that's what it is. You never made love so
            intensely before. It was as if it was going to be the
            last time.

MILDRED: Please don't say that George. It's...it's just that it
            was such a long time...

GEORGE: It wasn't such a long time.

MILDRED: It seemed long to me.

GEORGE: That's another thing. What happened last week
            we couldn't get together?

MILDRED: Nothing. Mama was getting suspicious, that's all.

GEORGE: I'm tired telling you, you worry too much.

MILDRED: I've stopped worrying. I just don't care anymore.

GEORGE: That's my girl. I only hope you mean it.

MILDRED: I do mean it.

GEORGE: *[He bends over and kisses her briefly]* Great. So we'll meet again tonight then?

MILDRED: Tonight? *[She says this in a strangely startled way, but checks herself]* Yes.

GEORGE: Same time? *[She nods her head. He goes to ask her something else but changes his mind]* Okay, I'll see you later then.

MILDRED: Ba-bye. *[On his way out he pauses to look at her. He seems to think all is not well. Eventually he shrugs his shoulders and exits. After he leaves she breaks down and cries]*

SARAH: *[Off stage]* Morning! Mildred! You wake yet? Mildred!

MILDRED: *[Pulling herself together]* I'm in the bedroom, Sarah. Come.

[Sarah enters]

SARAH: How you do?

MILDRED: Making out.

SARAH: You mean you no ready yet, girl? Come, go get ready.

MILDRED: What happen? You not working today?

SARAH: No, me dear child. That bitch Irma fire me.

MILDRED: For what? You and she get in something again?

SARAH: Not a thing. She just up and fire me like that.

MILDRED: What you going do, Sarah?

SARAH: I don't know yet. But don't let it hurt you head. Is Jesus Christ sharin' bread, not Irma Peebles. I hope you ain't tell George you going away?

MILDRED: No.

SARAH: That's good. Is the best ting you could do gel...Go to Canada wey you husban' is and start you life all over again.

MILDRED: *[About to break down again]* I can't go, Sarah. I just can't go.

SARAH: You young, Mildred. You would soon forget 'bout him. If you stop here things dead wid you. By the time that Irma Peebles get through pulling you name through the mud you wouldn't even be able to watch you own face in a lookin' glass. Is wha you crying for?

MILDRED: It's pointless, Sarah. I just can't go.

SARAH: Stop talking nonsense, girl. Is no point stopping here to mess up you life anymore. Pull yourself together and go get dress.

R BLOOD: *[Offstage]* Morning, Miss Mildred! You ready?

SARAH: She coming now. Just wait awhile.

            [Russia Blood enters]

R BLOOD: A wha you a do ya?

SARAH: Wha de ass you comin' in de gel bedroom for, Russia Blood?

R BLOOD: Eh, eh! So me can't come in a bedroom too?

SARAH: You ain't ha' no damn call in here. Go 'long back outside. *[She comes up threateningly to him. He ignores her]*

R BLOOD: Gel go gee youself peace, eh.

SARAH: Me say you no ha' no call in here, man.

R BLOOD: Look, is whey she going?

SARAH: That ain't you business.

R BLOOD: How come is not me business and is me have to
             drive she to where she going?

SARAH: Look, I say you don't have any call in here, and you
             don't have any call in here, so get out. *[Despite his
             protest she pushes him out. To Mildred]* We goin'
             pick up you mother and come back for you now,
             so get ready quick.

             *[As they leave, Mildred starts to cry again. She
             reaches for a bottle of pills and starts to swallow
             them as the lights go out]*

SCENE VIII

[Later that evening. Irma and Stanley enter from house]

IRMA: Did you check to make sure that she's gone?

STANLEY: *[He has been drinking but is not very drunk]* Irma,
             I have something more important to talk to you
             about.

IRMA: You're not going to bring up the divorce now I
             hope.

STANLEY: It's important that we get married soon!

IRMA: The Chief Minister is coming here for supper
             tonight.

STANLEY: You're not listening to me, Irma.

IRMA: I think it's good for mother to get together with her old friends, don't you? He should be here any minute now.

STANLEY: *[Not taking the hint]* After we're married, Irma, we can have her friends over every week.

IRMA: George should be here soon too.

STANLEY: Good. We could talk to him about the divorce then.

IRMA: *[Observing him carefully]* Have you started up that heavy drinking again?

STANLEY: I had to! *[Pause]* Life is rough, Irma.

IRMA: What new evidence do you have?

STANLEY: I'm tired, tired of being mocked by fate.

IRMA: Has something gone wrong?

STANLEY: Has anything ever gone right for me?

IRMA: You keep getting into these terrible moods. What is it now?

STANLEY: O'Brien has...Marry me Irma! Please marry me!

IRMA: Will you tell me what is wrong?

STANLEY: He's trying to ruin me, Irma. Don't you understand?

IRMA: Stop getting carried away and explain to me what has happened.

STANLEY: *[Pause]* I never mentioned this before, Irma, but the estate hasn't been doing too well financially. I needed money badly and there was this so-called

Canadian Company wanting land to buy. So, I sold some. But the company was...was just a front for...for...

IRMA: George? What's so ruinous about that? You needed money and you got it. Or didn't you?

STANLEY: That's not the trouble. He wouldn't let me harvest the cane crop I planted on the land. He's going to ruin me if you don't help me fight him, Irma.

IRMA: You sold him cultivated land?

STANLEY: I couldn't help it. My equipment broke down or I would have finished harvesting long before the deal was closed. It's not my fault. *[Pause]*Now he's trying to steal my crop. We can't let him do it, Irma. I spent a fortune on that sugar cane. It could ruin me.

IRMA: What are you going to do?

STANLEY: *[Pause. He sighs deeply]* I need a drink.

IRMA: This is no time for a drink. There must be something in the agreement that you can use to fight him with.

STANLEY: *[As if he hasn't heard her. As if indeed she isn't around]*Life is such a heavy burden. No justice, no mercy, no peace anywhere.

IRMA: This kind of talk isn't going to help matters.

STANLEY: Look at him. Everything he touches blossoms. Mushrooms into money. Success follows at his heels like a faithful dog. And then, look at me. Everything I put my hand to withers and dies as if destiny...God himself has decreed that I must meet with nothing in life but failure.

IRMA: That's your whole problem, Stanley! Can't you see? You've grown to believe this and so you've shut yourself off from everything but failure.

               [George enters from the garden eating a long piece of sugar cane]

STANLEY: Help me! You've got to help me, Irma. With your help I can do it.

IRMA: Hi, George.

GEORGE: Hi. He's here to complain me to you, too?

IRMA: Stanley dropped by to say hello.

GEORGE: How nice of him. *[To Stanley]* How's it going, old chap?

STANLEY: My visit doesn't exactly concern you.

GEORGE: Whatever goes on on my property concerns me. Like this lovely bit of cane I just broke from by land, for example. *[Stanley grimaces but remains silent]* Want some?

STANLEY: It's quite alright. You go ahead and enjoy it...while you still can.

GEORGE: While I still can? *[He laughs]* I hear you spreading a rumor that I'm trying to rob you.

STANLEY: Rumor? Well, I wouldn't exactly call it that myself.

GEORGE: So you're saying I'm a thief then?

STANLEY: That's not how I'd put it either. But I don't suppose your crude way of saying it makes it any less accurate.

GEORGE: Well, ole chap, the happy truth is that your sugar cane is now my sugar cane, just as your land is now my land. And all of your high-handed bullshit can't make that any less accurate.

STANLEY: Should I tell him, Irma? Or would you rather do it?

IRMA: Do what?

STANLEY: You tell him. Go on, tell him.

IRMA: Stanley!

GEORGE: Tell me what?

STANLEY: Irma and I have been discussing a serious matter for quite a while, O'Brien. I don't expect you'll be happy about it, but none the less that's life. We want you to know she intends to divorce you and marry me!

IRMA: Stanley! What on earth are you talking about? *[Trying to laugh it off]* He's been drinking, darling. Don't take him seriously.

STANLEY: Irma...!

IRMA: For heaven's sake, Stanley!

STANLEY: No...! You're joking! You've got to be!

IRMA: You're the one who's joking, Stanley.

STANLEY: You can't do this to me, Irma. You're not going to turn your back on me now?

GEORGE: Wait a minute...

STANLEY: For God's sake, Irma!

IRMA: Get a grip on yourself, Stanley!

STANLEY: For God in heaven's sake, Irma, PLEASE! Don't do this to me!

IRMA: Let me go, Stanley. Let me go! *[Stanley holds on to her]*

GEORGE: *[Intercepting and pushing Stanley away]* What the hell is wrong with you? *[Hustling him off]* Come on, you've made a big enough fool of yourself. Time to go.

STANLEY: *[Losing his temper and pushing George hard]* Don't push me! *[As George reapproaches him, Stanley picks up the cane George was carrying and they circle each other]*

IRMA: For heaven's sake! The Chief Minister is due here at any moment and I don't want you starting a brawl! George! Stanley! Stanley!

    [They ignore her. Stanley moves in firing vicious strokes with the cane which George easily eludes. They get into a clinch with the cane high above their heads. It becomes a stationary battle of strength with each seeking to possess the cane. George slowly forces Stanley to his knees, then eventually to the ground flat on his back. One of George's knees is now in Stanley's throat. Stanley continues to wrestle for a while. George merely keeps him pinned to the ground. Stanley's rage is now spent and there is no more fight in him. George gets up and throws the cane away. He pulls Stanley to his feet]

IRMA: Come on, George, maybe you'd better take him home and hurry back before the Chief Minister gets here.

STANLEY: I'll get home by myself. *[He walks away. On his way out he pauses and turns to Irma]* All my life I've loved you, Irma. If nothing else…if nothing else in this world, remember that. *[He exits]*

GEORGE: Start explaining.

IRMA: Well, it's just that. I've invited the Chief...

GEORGE: We'll get to that later. I want to know about this business of divorcing me and marrying him.

IRMA: I don't know what he's talking about.

GEORGE: So you expect me to believe that he made it all up?

IRMA: You know I seriously think he's gone off. The affair with the land and the cane and all that has him very upset. *[Pause]* You don't really believe I'd leave you for him, do you?

GEORGE: You never know.

IRMA: Well, I know! So let's go get ready to meet our guest.

GEORGE: The Chief Minister is coming for supper you said?

IRMA: That's what I'm trying to tell you. Both himself and Linton.

GEORGE: Why didn't you let me know before?

IRMA: I wanted it to be a surprise, darling. Linton is obviously not making much progress with getting you the hospital so I thought that you and I should speak to the Chief Minister personally.

GEORGE: The only problem is, I already have an appointment for tonight.

IRMA: Then cancel it!

GEORGE: I wish you'd let me know these things in advance, you know.

IRMA: Darling, I've gone through a lot of trouble to do this
            for you. The least you could do is show some
            appreciation.

GEORGE: Why is it that any time you so much as lift a straw
            you expect me to spend the rest of my life showing
            appreciation for it?

IRMA: Because you never do, George! I'm forever bend-
            ing over backwards for your benefit and you
            refuse to give me even the slightest amount of
            consideration.

GEORGE: Don't start with that again!

IRMA: Okay. *[Squaring her shoulders]* Where do you have
            to go to that's so important?

GEORGE: The amount of my money you waste on food and
            clothes alone would make Rockerfeller weep! And
            then you turn around and tell me that I am
            inconsiderate!

IRMA: Answer my question. What appointment do you
            have tonight?

GEORGE: I'm tired telling you, I'm not your son. Don't ask
            me questions like that.

IRMA: If you're such a big man, why don't you come right
            out and tell me you are planning to go and see
            Mildred Sweeney?

GEORGE: *[The directness of the question phases him for a
            while but he recovers quickly]* Alright. I am going
            to see Mildred. That makes you feel any better?

IRMA: I'll tell you what makes me feel better. I've seen to
            it that she's not around for you to see anymore.
            How does that make YOU feel?

GEORGE: What are you talking about?

IRMA: You think I was going to sit back and let her make a fool of me? You should know me better than that, George.

GEORGE: I'm not following you.

IRMA: I sent her packing to Canada this morning. ME!

GEORGE: You what?

IRMA: I got her papers from the Canadian Embassy, booked her flight, got her husband to send the ticket money and saw to it that she was off the island by today.

MRS. P.   *[From inside]* Irma, dear, our guests have just arrived.

GEORGE: *[To himself]* So that's why she was acting so strange.

IRMA: Keep them entertained until we come in, Mother. *[To George]* Don't let it upset you, darling. I had to do it, can't you see?

GEORGE: You figure you're tough, don't you?

IRMA: I had to do it, George. Surely you can see that. I had to do it for our sakes. She was getting in the way of our happiness. People were even beginning to laugh at me *[She tries to touch him but he pushes her away]* I'm the one who's supposed to be angry! I should be screaming my head off at you. But I've gotten her out of my way and I'm willing to let it die at that.

GEORGE: You sent her packing to Canada, so you proud of yourself. What good you think that's going to do?

IRMA: I just want us to live an ordinary peaceful life as a good husband and wife team, George, that's all.

GEORGE: Don't make me laugh.

IRMA: I love you, George.

GEORGE: You love the comfortable standard of living I give
             you.

IRMA: Is that what you think it is? I could have had a
             comfortable standard of living with Stanley, but
             it's you I love. It's you I want to be with.

             [Mrs. Peeples enters]

MRS. P: Irma, dear, you're keeping our guests waiting. The
             Chief Minister is asking for you.

IRMA: Will you please go back inside and be patient,
             Mother?

MRS. P: I hope you're not choosing this moment for an-
             other one of your quarrels.

GEORGE: Will you just get her back inside.

IRMA: Mother...please...

MRS. P.   The Chief Minister should not be kept waiting.

             [Sarah enters from the audience]

SARAH: Oh, George O'Brien...

IRMA: Where you do think you are going? Coming here
             to appeal to Mother and my husband is not going
             to do you any good. I've fired you and you're going
             to stay fired.

SARAH: Me ain't come here to beg you for a thing, you
             stinking bitch!

             [Linton enters]

LINTON: Easy! Take it easy. What's going on out here?

SARAH: You feel good that you was sending off Mildred to
            Canada? Well you almost sen' she to she grave, so
            you could feel even better now. That's all me come
            here to say.

IRMA: Well you've had your say now, so go on about your
            business. Go on before I send for the police to lock
            you up.

SARAH: Send for the police, nuh! Go ahead and send for
            the police! You must be think is Mildred you
            dealing with.

GEORGE: Wait a minute. What you saying, Sarah?

SARAH: Mildred in hospital, George O'Brien.

GEORGE: Hospital? What you mean hospital?

SARAH: Hospital! You don't know wha' that mean?

GEORGE: But...but what happen?

SARAH: You intrested? You really concern 'bout wha'
            happen to Mildred?

GEORGE: Yes I'm interested. And concerned.

SARAH: Well, she drink a whole bottle o' tablets. That a
            wha' you and da one dey *[indicating Irma]* drive
            she to.

GEORGE: How is she now?

SARAH: Critical.

GEORGE: Good God!

SARAH: Don't bother call pon God now. God done do his
            part, because she coulda dead. Now is up to me
            to do mine an' I go do it well. When you was in a
            position to help, all you was concerned 'bout was
            that you had another woman to sleep wid. But not
            any more. I done call Mildred husband and he
            making de arrangement for me to bring her up to

Canada as soon as she could travel. And for me to stay up dey in a Canada wid dem. *[To Irma]* So tek dat! Mildred Sweeney is me friend. Yes, Mildred Sweeney is my friend and as far as I concern is all o' you nearly kill she. And as for you George O'Brien, I hope you will get what you looking for from you chosen people before this bitch here drive you crazy!

[She exits. There is a long silence]

LINTON: Well, we can't stand here and stare all night. The Chief Minister is waiting.

MRS. P: I suppose you're right, Linton.

[They start moving off]

GEORGE: Good God! A woman almost killed herself. Doesn't that mean anything to anybody?

LINTON: Does it mean anything to you? Of course it does. It means something to all of us. But it's pointless to get worked up over it at this moment.

MRS. P: You're quite right, Linton. Besides we have kept the Chief Minister waiting long enough.

LINTON: Exactly. Come on, George. We have important matters to deal with.

GEORGE: Like what?

LINTON: Like getting the Chief Minister to convince London to use your designs for the new hospital.

GEORGE: Linton, you know and I know that's never going to happen.

LINTON: We have to try. And if anybody can persuade the British Government it's the Chief Minister. He's here now and willing to listen, so let's go talk to him.

GEORGE: You go talk to him.

IRMA: George...

GEORGE: Just get the hell away from me.

LINTON   George...

GEORGE: All of you.

LINTON: George, this is the best chance you're going to get.
             If all you want to do is build the hospital, fine. If
             you want your designs to be used, then let's go
             inside now.

GEORGE: If the C.M. asks for me, tell him I'm at the hospital.

             [He exits]

IRMA: George, please... *[She follows after him but Linton
             restrains her]*

LINTON: Let him go. He'll come back in his own time.

IRMA: But...but...suppose he doesn't?

MRS. P: Who cares? We'll raise a red flag. That's what we'll
             do.

IRMA: Mother, please...

LINTON: Don't worry, he'll be back. Sarah will take Mildred
             to her husband in Canada, and he'll have no place
             else to go but here.

IRMA: And the hospital?

LINTON: Very little chance, but it's up to you to try.

IRMA: Well...I'll do just that.

MRS. P: Come along now. We've kept the Chief Minister
             waiting long enough.

LINTON: Indeed. And I'm sure we can all use ourselves a
               drink.

               [They leave. The lights very slowly fade out]

                            THE END

For Better For Worse

For

Nicie, Eudora & Dahlia

For Better For Worse was first produced by the Montserrat Theatre Group as part of the Allioguana Arts Festival, Montserrat, on July 18, 1973, at the University Center. It was directed by the author, and earned him the award for best director that year, with the following cast:

SANDRA FORGERTY	Edith Kirnon
ANN FORGERTY	Irene Bramble
DEREK WELLINGTON	Gus White
ANDREW FORGERTY	Leslie Kelsick
JAMES WELLINGTON	Josephus Lewis
MOLLY	Glinnis Hunter
JOE	John O'Garro
CAROL	Jacquie Fredericks

Characters

SANDRA FORGERTY, *a young graduate teacher*

ANN FORGERTY, *her mother—a house wife*

DEREK WELLINGTON, *a university student—Sandra's boyfriend*

ANDREW FORGERTY, *Sandra's father—a top level civil servant*

JAMES WELLINGTON, *Derek's father—a minister of government*

MOLLY, *James' maid*

JOE, *a taxi driver*

CAROL, *a school teacher*

Setting

The play is set on Montserrat in the early 1970's.

SCENE ONE   **The Forgerty's living room**

The room is furnished somewhat better than the average middle income West Indian living room. Down left is an exit leading to the kitchen. Down right an exit leading to the bedrooms and up stage centre is the front door, leading to the street. There is a centre table, a couch, and an easy chair with a side table close by. A radio must be part of the set. There could also be a TV, side-lights, pictures making up the decor, but the stage should not be over-crowded.

SCENE TWO   **The Wellington's back veranda**

A veranda table and two or three veranda chairs. Left, a big "sleeping chair." Upstage a table with a telephone on it. A door leading into the house. Another door leading directly to James' bedroom. Entering from the audience is entering from the back yard.

SCENE THREE **The Forgerty's living room**

SCENE I

The Forgerty's living room.

When the lights come up the stage is empty. Sandra enters from bedroom [right] with a pile of exercise books. She walks over to the easy chair and places the books on the side table. Then she goes to the radio and switches it on. A "hot tune" is playing and she does a little dance as she goes back to the easy chair and sits. She starts marking books. In a little while, she puts down book and clutches her belly in pain. At this point Ann enters from kitchen.

ANN: I can't hear my ear in the place for all these benna songs, every minute.

          [She switches the dial to a religious station]

          There. Listen to something decent for a change. *[Looking at Sandra suspiciously]* You feeling bad again, Sandra?

SANDRA: *[Trying to brighten-up]* Oh no, Mommy. I'm just concentrating on what I'm doing. I'm trying to finish marking these books before Derek comes over.

ANN: Well, don't let me keep you.

          [She goes back into the kitchen, pausing at door to look at Sandra. Sandra goes back to marking books. In a short while she puts down the book, switches off the radio and lies down on the couch]

ANN: What you take it off for? *[Coming back in]* I want to listen. *[Walks to centre, turns to Sandra on couch]* You feeling sick again Sandra?

SANDRA: I'm alright, Mommy. Don't worry your head.

ANN: How you mean you're alright? I didn't know you're a doctor.

SANDRA: I don't feel so good, but it's nothing to make a big fuss about.

ANN: *[Coming over and examining her with hands]* Which part of you hurting you?

SANDRA: *[Pushing her off]* Just sit down and relax, Mommy. I tell you it's nothing.

ANN: I don't care what you say. If this goes on I'm calling Dr. O'Garro to look at you.

SANDRA: Oh Christ!

ANN: Something must be wrong with you. Last week you missed two days of school. Since when you ever missing two days of school in one week? You wouldn't eat a thing and you're so poory, it looks like you're withering away. I even had to ask them to pray for you at church.

SANDRA: *[Getting up]* Look here, Mommy. See? I told you I'll be alright. There's nothing wrong with me. I've been working hard and I'm just a little run down. That's all.

ANN: All I'm saying is that the best thing to do...

SANDRA: Okay, Mommy I'll visit the doctor, I'll visit the Doctor. *[Walks back to chair and sits]* Where's Daddy?

ANN: I couldn't tell you my child.

SANDRA: Isn't this his night for bridge?

ANN: Oh yes. He's probably out playing cards with Mr. Wellington. The Honorable James Llewellyn Wellington. I wonder if all these dreadful things people say about him could be true. You sure you feeling okay?

SANDRA: I'm fine, Mommy. What dreadful things?

ANN: The usual. How he's always interfering with his secretaries and things like that. And how he's going around now with some little girl half his age.

SANDRA: People always chatting about what's not their business. I'm sure nothing go like half the things they say.

ANN: Old people say you never see fire without smoke.

SANDRA: And if he even has a young girl, what's wrong with that? It might do him some good.

ANN: I don't believe it. I couldn't bring myself to believe such a thing about Mr. Wellington. *[Pause. She sits down in couch]* You think anything could go so for true?

SANDRA: Why don't you ask him when you see him again?

ANN: I can't do that! But Mr. Wellington is too much of a fine, upstanding man to be involved in that kind of thing, anyhow. And a good politician too. Just this morning they said on the radio that he's going to Guyana tomorrow. Just look at that. Going abroad to represent his island again, and at a big time conference on Federation besides. What a man. That son of his should be just a little more like him.

SANDRA: Why are you always picking on Derek?

ANN: I'm not picking on him. It's just that...

SANDRA: Just that what?

ANN: Well...I mean...Look how long he's going out with you and up to now he hasn't said a thing to me about his intentions. His father would never have done such a thing.

SANDRA: Times have changed, Mommy.

ANN: Well I think it's high time he let me know what he's
             about.

SANDRA: It's not you he's dating, you know.

ANN: What he said to you then? You're not getting any
             younger, you know. It's time you start to think
             about getting a husband. I hope Derek isn't just
             blocking traffic.

SANDRA: To tell you the truth, Mommy, we're not planning
             to get married.

ANN: What? I couldn't be hearing you right. No sensible
             girl is going to be running here and there with a
             man every minute, unless she planning to marry
             him.

SANDRA: Marriage isn't everything.

ANN: Every sensible woman wants to get married. What
             you want to be, an ole maid?

SANDRA: I'm surely not going to be any ole maid either.

ANN: Well, what you think is going to happen to you if
             you fool around now? You're not going to be young
             all your life.

SANDRA: You may as well start getting accustomed to the
             idea, Mommy. When Derek finishes university
             we're going to rent a house and just live together.

ANN: You mustn't joke about serious things like that
             you know, girl.

SANDRA: But I'm dead serious.

ANN: Dead serious?

SANDRA: Dead serious.

ANN: *[Getting up]*Dead crazy, you mean. *[Sandra smokes cigarette]* I tired tell you I don't want you smoking no cigarette in my house.

SANDRA: Okay, Mommy.

ANN: All this university education is corrupting the minds of you young people. How can you even think of such a thing? I told your father, "Andrew, I'm not in favor of sending Sandra to any university," and he wouldn't listen to me. Now look what happen. Just look what you have come to.

SANDRA: You're making it sound as if I'm some sort of a criminal. Me and Derek love each other, and that's the only thing that's going to keep us together. Not repeating a couple of stupid vows and signing a piece of paper.

ANN: So when he pick up and leave you, what you're going to do then? Who is going to work for you?

SANDRA: I'm an educated woman, Mommy. I don't need a man to work for me.

ANN: But you don't have any hold over him. He could fool around with any other woman he wants to.

SANDRA: I don't see the marriage vows stopping any of these married men today from fooling around. And some of the women too. Besides, if he is going to be free to fool around, then so am I.

ANN: You mean to tell me this is all the ambition you have, Sandra. All the ambition you have. To go and live in sin with a man?

SANDRA: *[Coming towards her]* Don't be upset, Mommy. It hasn't happened as yet and it's still a long way off. And there's something else I have to tell you too.

ANN: Well if it's anything like this I don't want to hear it. *[Sandra shrugs]* What is it?

SANDRA: Nothing serious. I'll tell you some other time. When you're not so upset.

ANN: Upset? Upset you call it? What has happened to all you've learned about the work of God, Sandra? Dear Jesus, what is the world coming to today? I hope you're still a virtuous young lady?

SANDRA: I'm 23 years old, Mommy!

ANN: So what? When I got married I was 24, and still as fresh as a blossom. Ask your father.

SANDRA: For heaven's sake, Mommy...*[She breaks off and clutches her middle]* Oh God! *[She rushes over and collapses on the couch]*

ANN: *[Alarmed and darting to her assistance]* Sandra! What's wrong, child? What's the matter with you?

SANDRA: *[Hardly able to talk]* Nothing. Just a cutting in my belly.

ANN: This thing is getting serious. *[She starts moving off]* Let me call...

SANDRA: *[Reaching out and grabbing her]* I'll be Okay in a little while. It's nothing.

ANN: Don't give me...*[The door bell cuts her off]* I'll see who it is.

            [Before she reaches the door, it is pushed open and Derek walks in]

DEREK: Hello, Mrs. Forgerty.

ANN: Oh, hello, Derek.

DEREK: How's life?

ANN: Not as good as you, my son. The pressure has been troubling me and you know I always suffer from dizziness.

DEREK: I thought you had gotten over the dizzy spells long ago.

ANN: Not at all. I still get them off and on.

DEREK: Anyway, you're looking as fit as a fiddle to me. *[He sees Sandra on couch]* Hey, Sandra.

SANDRA: *[Still a bit feeble]* Hi, Derek.

DEREK: What's the matter with you? *[He crosses from Ann to Sandra]* You're sick or something?

SANDRA: Just a pain in my belly.

ANN: I'm sure something is wrong with her. I was just going to call the doctor.

SANDRA: *[Sitting up, to Derek]* Don't worry with Mommy, eh. *[To Ann]* I told you I was going to see the doctor didn't I? It doesn't make sense to call him now.

DEREK: *[Sitting next to her]* What's there to eat? I'm as hungry as a dog.

SANDRA: What have you been up to?

DEREK: Been working out some new dance steps with the group.

SANDRA: I'll go see what's in the kitchen.

ANN: You sit down and relax, Sandra. I'll rustle up something. *[She leaves]*

DEREK: *[Getting closer to Sandra]* So what's going on?

SANDRA: Things don't look so good.

DEREK: What is that suppose to mean.

SANDRA: I think I'm pregnant.

DEREK: That's bad news. I was hoping you'd see your period by now. Maybe it will still come.

SANDRA: Well, it's two long months now. And I'm never late. Plus I've been vomiting and having all the usual sickness.

DEREK: That is bad news. Does your mother suspect anything?

SANDRA: I don't think so, but I can't keep it from her much longer. I've been sick often, and she's threatening to call the Doctor. I don't know how to tell her.

DEREK: *[Getting up thoughtfully]* Maybe that's not a bad idea. *[Turning to Sandra]* Calling the doctor I mean. Why don't you get the doctor to give you some tablets or something and take care of it? Then you wouldn't have to tell anybody anything.

SANDRA: I've thought of that, Derek. But I can't.

DEREK: *[Walking around back of couch]* Oh come on, Sandra, half the girls in town...

SANDRA: That is surely no reason why I should!

DEREK: *[Sarcastically]* Well...maybe you have some better ideas. *[Turns away]*

SANDRA: Why don't I just have the child?

DEREK: Don't be ridiculous.

SANDRA: *[Getting up]* I'm not being ridiculous. I'm serious. Why don't I just have the child?

DEREK: Look Sandra, we have agreed that marriage is out
             of the question. Apart from that I'm still at school.
             The time isn't right for any of that crap.

SANDRA: Who said anything about getting married? I'll
             have the baby, and by the time you finish univer-
             sity and we start living together, our family will be
             well on its way.

DEREK: You realise what you're saying?

SANDRA: Of course it's going to create a big scandal at first,
             and there'll be hassles with people like Mother,
             but it will all die down. Besides, I do want the
             baby.

DEREK: *[Chuckles a bit]* Sounds interesting. *[Thoughtfully]*
             I'm beginning to like the idea. *[Laughing outright]*
             Just imagine me being a Papa. *[They both laugh,
             and embrace each other]*

SANDRA: You can afford to laugh. I'm the one who's preg-
             nant.

             *[Ann has entered in time to hear the last of this.
             They realise she is in the room when the tray she
             is carrying crashes to the floor]*

ANN: Pregnant! Sandra, you pregnant! Oh my God,
             what is this for me at all. Lord Jesus what is this
             for me?

SANDRA: Don't work up yourself like that, Mommy. *[Picking
             things up]*

ANN: Who did this to you?

SANDRA: Oh Mommy, who else could it be. *[She takes tray
             to sideboard]*

DEREK: That's a good question.

ANN: How could you do such a thing Derek? After all the confidence we had in you these five years?

SANDRA: Please, Mommy...

ANN: You be quiet. I should have put my foot down on your nonsense long ago.

SANDRA: Well, it's too late to start now Mommy. Just relax.

ANN: Don't you have any shame girl? Think of what people are going to say. Our good name will be dragging in the gutters.

SANDRA: Oh, please...

ANN: That might not mean nothing to you, but think of me and your father.

SANDRA: There's nothing disgraceful about being pregnant, Mommy.

ANN: You have the nerves to watch me in my face and talk about no disgrace! Well, something has to be done about it.

SANDRA: Please Mommy, just leave...

ANN: The only thing that can save us now is for both of you to get married before the news gets around. *[To Derek]* I hope you know this means you will have to marry Sandra?

DEREK: Just leave it to us Mrs. Forgerty. We'll see to it that everything works out fine.

[James enters from the street immediately followed by Andrew]

JAMES: Hello my dear Ann. How're you doing? *[Examining her]* By God, you look like a million.

ANN: Oh, Mr. Wellington, it's so nice to see you. You and
            Andrew are just in time to hear the good news.

ANDREW: What good news?

ANN: Well...

JAMES: Come on, out with it, out with it.

ANN: Sandra and Derek are going to get married.

JAMES: Married!

ANDREW: Married?

JAMES: How the devil I haven't heard anything about this
            'till now?

ANN: They just decided suddenly. Tonight. Just now.

JAMES: I expected they would get married eventually and
            that it would be a grand occasion. But the damn
            boy is still...Wait a minute. The girl in trouble or
            something?

ANN: Shoo. Not so loud. You know how these young
            people blood hot.

JAMES: *[Turning to Derek and Sandra]* How in heavens the
            two of you could allow such a thing to happen?

DEREK: The usual way, Daddy. The usual way. *[Andrew
            chuckles]*

JAMES: *[Slightly annoyed]* This is no time for foolishness.
            We have to discuss the matter seriously.

ANN: One thing I know, the wedding will have to be soon
            to prevent any scandal.

JAMES: But of course.

DEREK: There isn't going to be any wedding.

ANN: But...but, there has to be!

ANDREW: Ann, Ann.

JAMES: Listen boy, you can't just walk into the home of a decent family like this, abuse their daughter and walk out as if nothing happen.

SANDRA: He hasn't abused me. I'm just as much responsible as he is. If not more so.

ANN: Sandra!

JAMES: That's beside the point. He still can't run out on you now.

SANDRA: What's the matter with all of you? He isn't running out on me. I'm going to have the baby, and when he's finished school we're going to live together.

ANDREW: Just like that?

JAMES: Young people today don't understand life.

ANDREW: If both of you plan to live together and raise a family, why not just get married and done?

DEREK: Because marriage is outdated and becoming more and more meaningless. We don't want any part of it.

ANN: But the word of the Lord...

ANDREW: Ann...Ann! Just go get us something to drink please.

ANN: That's the trouble with you, Andrew. You never want to hear anything about the word of God. [To James] That's the whole trouble with him.

JAMES: I'm quite sure my dear. A cold beer will do me fine. *[Still annoyed she turns to go. When she has made a few steps Andrew speaks]*

ANDREW: Bring one for me too.

ANN: *[Stopping but not looking around]* What about the rest of you?

SANDRA: Nothing for me, thank you.

DEREK: Nothing for me either. *[She leaves]*

ANDREW: Look, I know many marriages aren't perfect. Nothing is perfect.

DEREK: We know that too. But what about the marriage vows? Do they? They expect every marriage to be perfect. They ask you to pledge to stick with each other for better for worse, to love, honor and respect each other forever. How could any honest, sensible person make such a promise not knowing what's going to happen in five years, five months, five weeks? If two people should discover they're not compatible any more, what should they do? Live in misery for the rest of their lives as the vows ask, or separate in peace and try again? The thing is just ridiculous!

ANDREW: Fair enough. But in that event what is going to...

JAMES: *[Crossing in front of Andrew and coming closer to Sandra and Derek]* These children don't know what they're talking about. *[To Sandra]* Do you realise that this boy of mine will be able to take off and leave you anytime?

SANDRA: Nobody ever takes off and leaves a good thing. Besides, look how many husbands leave their wives, and wives leave their husbands. Marriage doesn't guarantee that all is going to go well. If our relationship is good, we'll find a way to work things out. If it isn't, then all the marriage vows in the world wouldn't help.

JAMES: You don't realise all that's involved. What's going to happen to the children? *[Ann comes in with beers]*

SANDRA: They'll be the same as any other children.

ANN: They'll be bastards.

JAMES: Do you realise that unless you are married the law offers little or no protection for you or for the child you're going to have?

SANDRA: That's a terrible shame. But none-the-less, what protection does the law give to children in a family where the parents are just staying together 'for the sake of the children.' What protection do children have from seeing their mother cry over and over again, because their father is out running around with someone of his...whores?

ANN: Sandra! Watch your language.

SANDRA: *[Brushing her aside with a wave of her hand]* If Derek and I are any kind of decent human beings, we'll make every effort to see that our children are adequately looked after without the force of the law, or the dubious merits of a marriage ceremony.

JAMES: That might sound good in theory, but what makes you think it can work?

DEREK: Marriage is a gamble, life is a gamble. Why should living together be any different? All we're saying is that a meaningful relationship has nothing to do with marriage vows or licence.

JAMES: Listen to me. This is a serious situation. Sandra is in trouble and going to live in sin is surely not the best solution to the problem.

ANN: Exactly!

JAMES: Derek, do you...

DEREK: Listen Daddy, I'm tired and hungry and I don't want to argue about it any more. Sandra and I are going out for a while so I can have something to eat and talk things over. *[They start to leave]*

ANN: *[Moving towards them]* You're not going any-where, Sandra.

ANDREW: *[Blocking her]* Leave them alone, Ann. *[They exit]*

ANN: That's the whole problem with you, Andrew. You spoiled her. You've always spoiled her. And look what happens now. She's going to disgrace the whole family. If you had listened to me and made her go to church...

ANDREW: Did going to church prevent you from becoming pregnant?

ANN: There's no need to bring up that now. Besides as soon as we realised our mistake, we got married and cleared it up.

ANDREW: Well I'm certainly not going to force them to get married.

ANN: We can't let them go through with it. Sandra having a bastard and living in sin! We can't let that happen, Andrew.

JAMES: I quite agree with you, Ann. Something has got to be done.

ANDREW: They're two sensible people. Just leave them to
             themselves and I'm sure things will work them-
             selves out.

JAMES: When you leave things to work themselves out,
             they never work out right. I'm a man who believes
             in making things work right.

ANN: So what we going to do then?

JAMES: Don't worry about it. Don't worry about it one little
             bit. *[He comes between them and rests his hand on
             one shoulder of each]* I'll take care of everything. As
             soon as I get back from Guyana, I'll see that
             everything is organized. After all, never let it be
             said that I, James Llewellyn Wellington, couldn't
             take care of a simple situation like this.

BLACK OUT

SCENE II

The back veranda of Mr. Wellington's house. Mid-morning.

When the scene opens, Molly is relaxing in the big chair. When she hears James shouting from inside, she jumps up and straightens herself, knocking over a bottle of beer she is drinking.

JAMES: *[From inside]* Anybody home? Derek! Molly! *[He enters just as Molly has scrambled to her feet. He is dressed in suit and tie and carries a briefcase]*

MOLLY: Oh is you, Sah. You frighten me. Me no me expect you so early.

JAMES: I can see that. You don't expect me so you lie down and cock up in my chair, eh?

MOLLY: Oh no, Sah!

JAMES: What's been happening since I've been away?

MOLLY: Not'ing at all, Sah.

JAMES: Where's Derek?

MOLLY: He left early and said he wouldn't be back till late. But me glad fu see you, sah. You look nice.

JAMES: This is the only place in the world I know where people expect to get money and don't work for it.

MOLLY: Wha' you saying, sah?

JAMES: You do any work for the day, Molly?

MOLLY: Of course, sah, plenty, plenty.

JAMES: You had better be right, or that beer comes out
            your pay at the end of the week.

            *[Joe enters carrying a suitcase. He has come
            around to the back so he walks on stage from in the
            audience]*

JOE: Where to put this, Sah?

JAMES: Leave it any place there. Molly will take it in. The
            wife and family keeping okay?

JOE: Everybody alright, Sah. An dem did tell me fu tell
            you howdy. De Madam going to de ground today
            so she will bring down some provisions for you.

JAMES: Good. Tell them I say howdy too. *[Turns to go]*

JOE: *[Clearing his throat to remind James that he has
            not been paid]* Er, er...Sah.

JAMES: Oh, I forgot that. *[Feels his pockets]* Check me out
            in the office tomorrow, Joe, and we'll straighten
            that out.

JOE: You no have nothing...

JAMES: Tomorrow!

JOE: Right-o, Sah. Me'll see you then. *[They both turn
            to go. Joe hesitates until James is inside, then
            turns back]* So what's going on Molly?

MOLLY: Me just a tek it easy, boy.

JOE: You looking well sweet and nice. *[He tries to touch
            her]*

MOLLY: No get fresh wid me eh, boy!

JOE: Wha' wrong wid you tall? You mean me can't
            touch you no more?

MOLLY:	Why you no go touch you wife?
JOE:	But if me touch me wife alone all de time me soon get fed-up.
MOLLY:	Well, no come touch me.
JOE:	You well up pan you high hoss today. No tell me dat is de boss touching you up now.
MOLLY:	A wha' you a say tall.
JOE:	Me know he sharp lek a razor blade.
MOLLY:	Well, he better no come play no fool wid me either. Me gat me man.
JOE:	So dat is why you getting on so these days. You nar bother wid me at all at all.
MOLLY:	You a somebody fu badder wid?
JOE:	You no even self gee me the latest flash.
MOLLY:	Me no know wha' you a talk bout.
JOE:	No tell me you no hear how Derek breed off Mr. Forgerty daughter?
MOLLY:	A wha' you a say tall? Me no hear a thing.
JOE:	A joke you a gee.
MOLLY:	Me nar joke, me no hear nuttn.
JOE:	Well, it all over town, gel.
MOLLY:	When you nose right in a de pot you never could smell, for true. Anyway de two of them could just get married and done. Dem a friend long enough.
JOE:	Dat a de trouble gel. Derek say he nar get married.

MOLLY: So you mean he jus' me a fool arf de poor gel all this time? Ah you man really worthless for true, sah.

JOE: You no begin to hear nothing yet.

MOLLY: Well me a listen.

JOE: Mark you, no go say me say.

MOLLY: You know me wouldn't even tell me own mother.

JOE: Gel dem gat big bacchanal down a de Forgerty house de other night. Mrs. Forgerty collar up Derek and shake he out and ask he wha' he intend to do 'bout she daughter.

MOLLY: For true, for true?

JOE: Me nar lie you. De woman get bad. She rant and rave and cuss, but all de carry on she carry on, Derek still decide he no in a nothing wid no wedding.

MOLLY: A wha' me a hear ya tall!

JOE: Wait man, me a tell you how it go. Things get so bad, dem have to send for de big Boss.

MOLLY: Mr. Wellington?

JOE: Mr. James Llewellyn Wellington himself.

MOLLY: Me a tell you.

JOE: And from the time de big boss hit de scene, everything cool. He tell Derek he have to come better than that.

MOLLY: De boss no easy for true.

JOE: You're tell me. But me hear just tidday self that Derek still a say he no in a nuttn wid no marriding.

MOLLY: So wha' a go happen?

JOE: Derek feel that he tough, but he will soon see who
            tough. Anyway gel, me have to mek a fast trip to
            the airport, so me rushing off now.

MOLLY: But you no done tell me how de story go.

JOE: Me can't stop now. But why you don't let me pick
            you up later and we could talk about it?

MOLLY: A smart you a play?

JOE: No, gel. Wha' you a go on wid. A we could discuss
            de whole ting later and me will gee you all de
            details.

MOLLY: Well...Well, alright then. Me see you later.

JOE: Keep you mouth shut now.

MOLLY: No worry 'bout that man. Take it easy.

            *[He leaves. She immediately goes to the phone and
            dials]*

            Bella, ah you dat? Me got one bone fu pick wid
            you. How come you no gee me de latest gist?
            Yes...dat a what me a talk 'bout. Gel me no hear
            a thing meself till today. What a thing pan God
            earth for true? Mrs. Forgerty pickney breed arf!
            Me agree wid you gel, it serve she just right. Yes,
            yes, you right wid dat. De 'ole gel so science wid
            she self, she no even does tell neaga howdy. Derek
            should never piss pan she. A so me hear gel!
            Dardy-oh, since me barn... *[Laugh]* Look, it sound
            lek de mister coming, so me have to go. But a we
            got to go pound story pan dat later. See you.

            *[James reappears. He has changed his clothes
            and is looking fresh and relaxed]*

JAMES: I thought I heard Joe out here still.

MOLLY: He just left Sah.

JAMES: He wanted something?

MOLLY: He was trying to get fresh wid me, Sah, so I had to
                put him in his place.

JAMES: Well, that's the two of you business. Go bring me
                a beer or something. *[As she passes him he slaps
                her on the rear]* You have a good little ass here, you
                know.

MOLLY: You better behave you self, eh.

                *[She exits. James sits down and is leafing through
                his newspaper, when Molly reappears]*

                A nice young lady out there to see you, Sah.

JAMES: Who is it?

MOLLY: I don't know she name, Sah, but is de same one
                you had last week.

JAMES: Show her in...who ever the devil it may be.

CAROL: *[Carol enters from house. She is about 28 and
                nicely dressed]* I'm in already, Romeo.

JAMES: *[Jumping up]* Oh; Carol, it's you! How're you doing
                honey bunch? Come on over here let me have a
                look at you. *[He looks her over]* Man, you're looking
                good enough for a king.

CAROL: You really think so?

JAMES: Bet your life I do.

                *[He hugs her and tries to kiss her, but she stiffens
                as Molly is looking at all this with eager eyes.
                James frowns at her]*

What are you hanging around for?

MOLLY: Are…er…

JAMES: Never mind. Take the rest of the day off.

MOLLY: But what about the beer, Sah?

JAMES: Just disappear, Molly. *[She exits]* Make sure you're early tomorrow. *[He leads Carol over to one of the chairs, pulls up one close to her and sits on it]*

CAROL: Why did you send her away?

JAMES: *[Putting his hand around her in an intimate way]* Well, why do you think?

CAROL: *[Resisting him]* I can't stay very long.

JAMES: It's been a whole long week since I saw you last.

CAROL: That's true, but I just dropped in for a few minutes. I heard on the radio you had a successful trip and was back early, so I just passed to see how you were.

JAMES: Well, what's the big hurry?

CAROL: I've got so many things to do. First of all, I have to pick up a dress at the seamstress and take it to show Sandra. And then…

JAMES: That can't prevent you from spending a little time with me.

CAROL: Tonight, James. Then you can take me to Vue Pointe and we can have a real swing.

JAMES: Tonight is a long way off. Up to now you haven't even kissed me. *[She puts her arms around his neck and is about to kiss him when Ann calls from inside]*

ANN: Mr. Wellington, Mr. Wellington dear! *[She enters]* Are you...*[She stops dead as she sees them in each other's arms. The grimace which passed over James face changes into a smile]*

JAMES: Oh Ann, how nice to see you.

ANN: I hope I'm not interrupting anything. I didn't realise you were busy.

CAROL: It's alright, I was just leaving. Don't forget tonight, dear.

JAMES: Not at all. Take it easy now. *[She exits]*

ANN: Who is that girl?

JAMES: You don't know her?

ANN: No.

JAMES: Of course you do. That's one of the new teachers from Trinidad. Carol Summersdale. She's Sandra's friend.

ANN: Oh, so that's her. I hear Sandra speaking about her all the time but I've never met her. Well, she certainly hasn't wasted any time.

JAMES: You can say that again.

ANN: And you. You're just as bad a wolf as they say.

JAMES: You better watch out that this bad wolf doesn't eat you up. You're a fine looking woman, you know.

ANN: You ought to be ashamed of yourself, Mr. Wellington. Fooling around with a little girl like that. She could almost be your daughter.

JAMES: Ann my dear, instead of scolding me, why don't you help me to correct my wrong doings.

ANN: Would, would you like me to pray with you?

JAMES: Oh, no.

ANN: Well, how can I help you then?

JAMES: By letting me fool around with you instead.

ANN: You wouldn't dare!

JAMES: *[Laughing]* Oh no, no, no. Of course not. I'm only pulling your leg. *[He shows her to a chair and they both sit]* Well, did you want to see me for something special?

ANN: Er...yes, yes. About the wedding.

JAMES: Oh yes, of course. I'm looking after it. Don't worry.

ANN: I am a bit worried. Nobody has said a thing to me and people are starting to talk. Plus the church...

JAMES: Don't worry about it. Now that I'm back everything will be looked after.

ANN: I know that you would take care of things. Andrew wouldn't lift a finger.

JAMES: I'm sure he's only busy with his work.

ANN: You don't know Andrew. Oh well. *[Pause]* But you're still quite a young man yourself. Why don't you get married again?

JAMES: Well, my dear, Dorothy's memory, bless her, is
              still very near and dear to me. So I imagine it
              would be quite some time before I can even think
              of such things.

ANN: It's over a year now since she passed away, isn't
              it?

JAMES: Yes, but I still think that's too soon.

ANN: You're such a considerate man. Giving her due
              honor and respect even in the grave. Andrew
              would never do such a thing for me.

JAMES: Oh I'm quite sure he would.

ANN: You don't understand. Nobody understands.

              *[She turns away. He suddenly reaches out, grabs
              her and kisses her. For a brief moment, her hand
              reaches up as if she is going to embrace him, then
              she pulls away and jumps up]*

              Don't do that. If the church should...

JAMES: *[Getting up right after her]* The church, the church,
              the church! Everything is the church. We have to
              give vent to our feelings, Ann. *[He tries to embrace
              her]*

ANN: No. Wait! I've never done anything like this before.

JAMES: Of course you haven't. *[Under his breath]* It's
              always the first time. Listen Ann, we are only
              human. The Lord will understand and forgive.

              *[He embraces her again. This time she allows
              herself to be embraced. Just as he is about to kiss
              her, she pulls away her head]*

ANN: People might pass and see us.

JAMES: What people? There're no people around.

ANN: *[Pointing to the audience]* Who are those?

JAMES: Those don't matter. They don't know who we are.

ANN: Are you sure?

JAMES: Of course I'm sure. Besides they're minding their own business.

[They embrace and kiss. While they are still holding each other, James eases her over to the big chair. Just as they have both slipped onto the chair, James lying on Ann, Derek is heard off stage]

DEREK: Dad! Daddy! Are you outside?

[At the sound of Derek, both James and Ann jump to a sitting position. James quickly forces Ann to stand up. When Derek enters, James is lying in the chair with one hand gripping an arm of the bewildered Ann, who is standing over him. James lets off a groan, looks up and speaks to Ann in a feeble voice]

JAMES: I think I'll be alright now, Ann. If you just step inside and get me two aspirins I'll be able to manage.

ANN: *[Badly shaken]* Er...yes, yes, Mr. Wellington.

JAMES: Oh Derek. It's you?

DEREK: What on earth...

JAMES: My trip must have worn me out more than I expected. If it wasn't for Ann, I might have passed right out.

[Ann, who has started for the door very unsteadily, swoons. Derek catches her before she hits the ground]

DEREK: This passing out business seems to be catching. Help me get her over to the chair. *[They both lift her over to the chair]* What's this? Some kind of fainting epidemic or something?

JAMES: This thing looks serious. I can't understand it. If she wasn't here I might have fallen and injured myself. And now look at her.

DEREK: I'm looking. You want me to call the Doctor?

JAMES: No, no. It's not that serious.

DEREK: How do you know?

JAMES: It can't be anything serious.

DEREK: What have you been doing to the poor woman, Dad?

JAMES: What do you mean, 'What have I been doing to the woman?' Nothing! We were just there talking, then all of a sudden I almost passed out. Well don't look at me that way. You think I'd lie to you.

ANN: What happened? Where am I?

JAMES: *[Moving towards her]* Easy now Ann, easy. *[He changes his mind]* You better look after her.

DEREK: Okay, Mrs. Forgerty, there's nothing to worry about. You must have had one of your spells. I'll take you inside and get you something to drink and put you to lay down so you can rest for a while. *[He puts one of her arms over his shoulder and takes her out]*

JAMES: What the hell is this for me at all? When is not one damn thing is the next.

            [Carol enters from back yard]

CAROL: You're still here, darling? Good. I was hoping you hadn't taken off on one of your many little missions.

JAMES: Carol, I thought...

CAROL: Yes, but I changed my mind. Decided to spend some time with you after all. *[She gives him a peck on the cheek]* Well, aren't you glad?

JAMES: Oh yes, of course, of course. Only I'm so busy right now. I've got some business to talk over with Derek.

CAROL: I thought Derek was out.

JAMES: He got back just a few minutes ago. So while we're here together for a change, I might as well grab the chance to talk over things with him.

CAROL: That's okay. Go right ahead and talk. I'll just slip into the kitchen and cook you both some roti and curried chicken. How's that? *[Derek enters]*

JAMES: Oh no, no. I couldn't let you do that. Why don't you drop over and see Sandra as planned, and I'll pick you up later and take you to View Pointe for dinner.

DEREK: Did I hear roti?

CAROL: *[Turning to Derek whose presence was not noticed until now]* I think your father is trying to get rid of me. Okay, Derek, I'll cook just enough roti for you.

DEREK: That's just fine with me, baby.

JAMES: Okay, okay. Make it. But I don't think you should go through all that trouble.

CAROL: No trouble at all. *[She exits]*

JAMES: I hope you realise what you might be getting me
            into.

DEREK: Me?

JAMES: What you think she's going to think when she sees
            Ann here?

DEREK: What is there for her to think?

JAMES: You know women.

DEREK: Don't worry about it, Dad. Besides, if she doesn't
            go into your bedroom, she'll probably not see Ann
            at all.

JAMES: Into my bedroom!

DEREK: Well, that's where the closest bed was.

JAMES: She's got to be moved. *[He hurries off]*

DEREK: No Dad, wait. *[He hurries after James]*

CAROL: *[She enters with two bottles of beer in her hands]*
            These should help to keep you two boys...James!
            Derek!

JAMES: *[From inside]* We're coming.

CAROL: *[She places beer on table]* I brought you two some
            beer. It's on the table. *[She turns to go but sees
            James' suitcase]* I'd better take this in and unpack
            it when I get a chance. *[She exits]*

DEREK: *[He enters, bringing James with him]* What's the
            matter with you? You can't go and arouse her
            now. You'll just upset the woman all over again.

JAMES: Okay, okay. You've made your point.

DEREK: *[Grabbing a beer]* Carol brought us some beer.
            [Gives one to James]

JAMES: Good. I could use a drink. *[Takes a long drag]* I didn't even get a chance to compliment you on your performance the other night.

DEREK: What performance?

JAMES: The way you handled the little situation over by the Forgerty's. Evading the issue of marriage. You know what I mean. Cornered but playing for time. Temporizing like a true diplomat. Brilliant. But there's nothing to worry about. Your Dad will get you out of the little jam.

DEREK: I don't think I quite read you, Dad.

JAMES: We both know you can't afford to get married now. You've got your studies to think about first.

DEREK: I have no intentions of getting married.

JAMES: Exactly. So I'll arrange to have Dr. Walcheck take care of the girl. You know what I mean. *[Derek attempts to speak but is cut off]* Of course the mother is going to be a little upset about this. But I'll make her see that it's the best thing for the time being. After you get out of school, you could get married then.

DEREK: Listen Dad, your friend Dr. Walcheck isn't going to take care of anything.

JAMES: *[Already on his way to the phone]* I'll just get on the phone...Now wait a minute! What did you say?

DEREK: You heard me. I said your friend Dr. Walcheck isn't going to take care of anything.

JAMES: Now let me make sure I get this clear. The girl is with child?

DEREK: Um-huh.

JAMES: She's going to keep the child?

DEREK: Um-huh.

JAMES: And you're not going to marry her?

DEREK: Right.

JAMES: You're not going to tell me that you were really serious about all the shit you were shooting the other night?

DEREK: You know, Dad, you're right again. Go to the head of the class.

JAMES: Come on Derek. You have to have more sense than that. You know you can't do such a thing. Look. If you and Sandra want to have a child, fine. It's about time I had some grandchildren anyway. True you're young and still in university and all that, but there's nothing wrong with settling down while you're young. I'd hardly turned twenty when I married your mother myself. We'll have a big wedding and settle everything.

DEREK: A big wedding, a big party, a big spree. The answer to all your problems. The best solution to every pregnancy.

JAMES: What have you got against marriage anyway?

DEREK: I'm tired of going over that.

JAMES: And what about Sandra? What does she feel?

DEREK: You know she feels the same way about it as I do.

JAMES: If you believe that, then you're an even bigger fool than I thought. There's no such thing on earth as a woman who doesn't want to get married.

DEREK: We'll see.

JAMES: Listen son. The Forgerty's are a decent and respectable family. You can't expect Sandra to go an have a bastard like some...common country girl?

DEREK: You see how you think? It's all well and good for some 'common country girl' to have a bastard child, which she cannot afford. But no such disgraceful behavior from the daughter of a decent respectable family! I suppose it is decent and respectable to throw away the child?

JAMES: That's besides the point.

DEREK: No it isn't.

JAMES: Arguing isn't going to get us anywhere. Do me a favor and marry the girl. Elections are next year and a scandal like this could be harmful to me. And, after all, what's harmful to me is also harmful to you.

DEREK: You really think people worry about the private lives of you politicians? If they did, which one of you would ever stand a chance of getting elected to office?

JAMES: I agree that some of these young fellows don't have any discretion. But give them a chance, they'll see.

DEREK: They're not going to see a thing. The people have always been aware of the way you older guys carry on. You think they're stupid.

JAMES: That might be so. But it's not what you do, it's how you do it. If people think you're trying to be discrete they would look away. On the other hand, if you're too brazen...

DEREK: Tell you what Dad, you concern yourself with what you do and how you do it in office. That is what is going to determine whether or not you get back in power. Not how I choose to live my life.

CAROL: *[Rushing in and confronting James]* So that's what it is, eh? That is why you didn't want me around!

JAMES: Oh, Christ! Let me explain...

CAROL: I don't want to hear anything. I saw her. It's not anybody tell me this time. And if I didn't take in your suitcase to unpack it I would never have known. *[He tries to put his arms around her. She screams]:* Don't touch me! I've had more shit from you than I'm prepared to take and I'm damn sick and tired of it. *[She storms off]*

JAMES: Women! Goddam women! Why the hell can't anything go right with them?

DEREK: Quite a hot Mama that one. If you're so anxious for a wedding, why don't you marry her?

JAMES: Forget about her. Forget the hell about the bitch and let's get back to our affairs.

DEREK: It's a waste of time, Dad. I'm just not going to get married.

JAMES: Don't tell me it's a waste of time. I say you marry the girl and that's final.

DEREK: Relax, Dad. You're losing your cool.

JAMES: The amount of things you've put me through would make the North Pole lose its cool. But not any more, Derek. Not one damn.

DEREK: What are you working up yourself so for? Listen, Daddy, try and understand...

JAMES: How long do you expect me to go on trying to understand? When you finally decided to go to university, I told you study law, study political science, study medicine, something useful. No, you want to study sociology. Alright, I agree. I send you to Canada. Instead of going up there, keeping your tail quiet and learning your lessons, what you do? You go get yourself mixed up with that Douglas fellow and those other hooligans, and burn the people's university down. All of that I take. And now you want to embarrass and humiliate me again? Well not this time my friend. Not this time.

DEREK: There're some things that people like you with your colonial mentalities will never be able to understand.

JAMES: I don't want to hear any of that shit. Colonial mentality, or colonial mentality not, around here, what I say still carries.

DEREK: What are you trying to do? Force me to get married or something?

JAMES: All I'm saying is to make up your mind what you're doing by tonight. And if you can't see things my way, then take your belongings and find some place else to go. *[Derek shrugs, James starts walking off then swings back]* And you might as well forget about me paying the rest of your way through school. *[He storms off]*

DEREK: *[Calling out to him]* Daddy! *[The door slams]* Shit! What the hell is a man to do? *[Sandra enters]*

SANDRA: Derek, what was that about? All the shouting?

DEREK: Just a quarrel with the old man.

SANDRA: Well, I gathered that much...

DEREK: Then why the hell are you asking me stupid questions? *[He walks away down right]*

SANDRA: Hey, I'm not the old man you know. Don't go lashing out at me. *[Silence. She walks over to him]* Come on Derek, snap out of it. *[She tries to tickle him. He pushes her away]*

DEREK: I'm just not in the mood for playing around, Sandra.

SANDRA: Well, tell me what happened then. *[He walks over to the left and sits on one of the chairs. She moves a few steps towards him]* Well?

DEREK: I just got kicked out of the house and my tuition fees have been cut off.

SANDRA: Why would James want to do a thing like that?

DEREK: He's trying to muscle me into getting married.

SANDRA: Derek? *[She rests her right hand lovingly on his right shoulder, moves slowly around the chair and sits down on his left knee with her arm over his shoulder]* Wouldn't it be simpler it we just get married?

DEREK: *[Pushing her off and jumping up in one motion]* No! That's absolutely out of the question.

SANDRA: *[Offended]* Surely Derek, there's no need for you to get fanatical about it. Mother is so upset about the whole thing, that if we don't get married I'm sure she's going to lose her mind. And now this thing with your father. You know how pig-headed he is.

DEREK: That's the whole point. You don't expect me to have the old man pushing me around and telling me how to live my life?

SANDRA: But it all seems such a great big pointless struggle.

DEREK: That's life. *[Silence]*

SANDRA: Derek. *[She walks slowly over to him and puts both arms around his neck]* Do you love me?

DEREK: Of course I do.

SANDRA: Well why are you so against marrying me? Am I not good enough to be your legal wife? *[He laughs. She withdraws her arms]* What's so funny?

DEREK: I'm just laughing about something Dad told me about every woman wanting to get married. Look Sandra, we have plenty of time to quarrel. Right now, we should be sticking together.

SANDRA: You still haven't answered me. *[Pause]* Well are you going to marry me?

DEREK: No, I'm not.

SANDRA: Oh, really? So that's how it is? *[She turns quickly and starts to hurry off. He runs and grabs her]*

DEREK: Come on, Sandra. You know I'm head over heels in love with you. How could I ever think of marrying you and have marriage turn you into a fat and peevish old lady within a few years?

SANDRA: *[Laughing in spite of herself]* Oh, Derek, you're such a scream. *[She embraces him. They laugh and kiss]*

DEREK: Nothing like a good bit of loving to take a man's mind off his troubles. But I'm afraid I'm still in the same rut. *[He flops down in one of the chairs]* Well, I guess I'll just have to find myself a permanent job and forget about school for the time being.

SANDRA: No Derek. That will never do. We're in this together. And with you working part time and me working all year round, we should be able to manage the fees.

DEREK: *[He pulls her into his lap and kisses her]* You know, if I ever decide to get married, you're the first on my list. Come help me pack. *[He picks her up in his arms and walks out with her]*

[The lights fade slowly until the stage is quite dimly lit. Then Ann enters]

ANN: Derek. Mr...Mr. Wellington. Nobody seems to be here. Well, look what a mess I nearly get myself in. *[She crosses herself]* Never me again!

BLACK OUT

SCENE III

The set is the same as Scene I. It is late afternoon. When the lights come up the stage is empty. The front door opens and Andrew walks on with his briefcase. He rubs his eyes. From the bedroom Sandra shouts.

SANDRA: Is that you, Dad?

ANDREW: Yes.

SANDRA: *[Entering]* Only now you coming from work or you were out liming?

ANDREW: Straight from work. And I'm dead beat.

SANDRA: *[Taking briefcase]* Here, let me take this in for you. *[From inside]* You want your slippers, Dad?

ANDREW: Thanks. *[He goes over to the liquor cabinet and pours himself a drink, then relaxes in the couch]*

SANDRA: *[Returning]* So, what have you been up to?

ANDREW: I was working on a speech for James and that held me. *[He rubs his eye]*

SANDRA: Something in your eye.

ANDREW: It's been bothering me all afternoon. As if sand or something is in it.

SANDRA: Let me see. *[She looks into the eye]* I don't see anything. Hold on. *[She blows into the eye]* How's that?

ANDREW: It's so sore that I don't even know.

SANDRA: Come again. *[She blows again]*

ANDREW: Okay, let that do. I'll see in a while if it's any better.
               How was your day?

SANDRA: So, so.

ANDREW: Problems?

SANDRA: Well, yes.

ANDREW: Any new developments?

SANDRA: None that I know of, but I'm expecting Carol to
               stop by any time now. She says she has some-
               thing important to tell me.

ANDREW: Maybe old James has finally proposed.

SANDRA: That would be the day. She hinted that it was
               something to do with Derek and me.

ANDREW: How are things going in that direction?

SANDRA: I don't know what to say, Dad. It's all so frustrat-
               ing. Everyone is getting on so funny, and well, you
               know for yourself how Mommy is behaving.

ANDREW: It takes a lot of courage for a single woman to have
               a child in our society. And going to live common
               law with Derek isn't going to make things any
               better.

SANDRA: I know that Dad, and I'm beginning to wonder if
               all this stress and strain is worth it. *[Pause]* Up to
               now Derek has not been given any explanation for
               why he was fired from his holiday job and now
               nobody else will employ him. It's all so...so...it just
               gets me down.

ANDREW: Why don't you just get married and done?

SANDRA: We can't do that, Dad.

ANDREW: Why not?

SANDRA: We decided long ago that we'd live together without getting married, and we're not going to change that now.

ANDREW: Even though the pressure against you is becoming unbearable?

SANDRA: We're not going to let society dictate our way of life.

ANDREW: It's impossible to live in a society and not have that society dictate your way of life.

SANDRA: Daddy, I'm not in the mood for any philosophical arguments right now. And in any case, if I even wanted to get married, Derek is dead set against the idea.

ANDREW: Well the two of you are two young people. You will have to find a way to work things out. Where's your mother?

SANDRA: Gone to one of her church meetings I believe. You're hungry?

ANDREW: No, I'm okay.

SANDRA: *[The door bell rings]* That must be Carol now. Answer for me please, Dad. *[She takes Andrew's shoes into Bedroom. Andrew answers the door. It is Carol]* Hi, Carol. Come on in.

CAROL: Hello Mr. Forgerty. Nice to see you.

ANDREW: Nice to see you too. Come right in and have a seat. Sandra will be out in a minute.

CAROL: Thank you.

ANDREW: Care to join me with a brandy?

CAROL: Not right now thanks.

ANDREW: Something softer then?

CAROL: Nothing at all at the moment.

SANDRA: Hi, Carol. You met Dad before, didn't you?

CAROL: Oh yes. We're quite old friends. Only your mother
             I haven't met as yet.

SANDRA: Well you'll meet her this afternoon. She's out now
             but she should be back soon.

CAROL: Good. I'm looking forward to it.

ANDREW: So how are things going with you, Carol?

CAROL: Not so good recently, to tell the truth.

ANDREW: What happen, ole James not behaving himself?

CAROL: You might say so.

ANDREW: That no-good rascal.

CAROL: Would you believe I went to see him the other day
             and he had a woman in his bed?

ANDREW: *[Laughs heartily]* That's just like James. What did
             the sun-of-a-gun have to say for himself?

CAROL: If he even had anything to say I didn't want to
             hear. I wash my hands. I'm done with that!

SANDRA: That would really serve him right for true. It's just
             what he deserves.

ANDREW: Oh, you'll get over it.

CAROL: Not this time. I've had it up to here. *[Puts hand to
             neck]* And I'm not taking any more shit from him.

ANDREW: That's what you say now, but you'll get over it.

CAROL: I don't think so. When I decide to give myself to a man, it is to that man, and that man alone. And I expect the same thing in return. No. I demand the same thing in return, and if he's not prepared to give it, then he doesn't deserve me.

ANDREW: But surely you must have known that Don Juan, Cassonova and James Llewellyn Wellington are all in the same league.

CAROL: Well, it was just hearsay. And he kept giving me the assurance there was nobody else.

ANDREW: He gave you that assurance?

CAROL: Honest to God.

ANDREW: Well, why am I pretending to be surprised?

CAROL: So I went to see him one day, the same day he came back from Guyana, and he seemed happy to see me, wanted me to spend the afternoon with him and all that, but this woman, an older matured lady came by and I left. I came by to see Sandra, but nobody was here so I went back. All of a sudden he's no longer happy to see me. He's making every excuse to get me to leave. But I stayed and happened to go into his bedroom, and there sprawled off in his bed is this same woman.

ANDREW: Who was the woman?

CAROL: I don't know and I don't want to know. All I know is that I felt like strangling her.

SANDRA: You should have strangled him.

CAROL: Right. So before I ended up with blood on my hands, I got out of there and out of the relationship in a lot of hurry.

ANDREW: Anyway, I know you girls have other business to
            talk over so I'll get out of your way and let you get
            on with it.

SANDRA: No, Dad, stay. I want him to hear what's happen-
            ing, Carol, okay?

CAROL: Sure.

SANDRA: So what's going down?

CAROL: Girl, I don't even know where to start. You know
            that old Teacher Alice who I live with is on the
            school board, don't you? Well she told me today
            that the board had a special meeting last night to
            discuss the situation with you and Derek.

SANDRA: Really? What they say?

CAROL: Don't say I told you, but they decided to ask for
            your resignation.

SANDRA: Oh my God! But why? On what grounds?

CAROL: You know how those old people think. She said
            your getting pregnant is bad enough, but going to
            live in sin with Derek makes it even ten times
            worse. Plus you know they have to talk about
            what a bad influence you will be on the children
            and that kind of thing.

SANDRA: Those old conceited, self-righteous, ass holes!
            Isn't there anything I can do Dad?

ANDREW: Like what?

SANDRA: To stop them from doing it. To fight them!

ANDREW: I really don't know, my dear. I would suggest you
            call Derek and tell him about it.

SANDRA: I don't see how that is going to help.

ANDREW: Well, it's his problem just as much as yours. Both of you work it out together.

SANDRA: *[A little annoyed]* Okay, if that's the way you feel, we'll work it out ourselves. *[She exits]*

CAROL: Why don't they just get married?

ANDREW: Maybe they realise marriage isn't as glorious as it is supposed to be.

CAROL: They could at least give it a try.

ANDREW: They want to try something else.

CAROL: But they could see how other people here feel about that. How are they going to get it to work? *[Andrew rubs his eye again]* Is there something in your eye?

ANDREW: Yes, I think so. It's been bothering me all afternoon but whatever it is I can't seem to get it out.

CAROL: Just a minute, I'll take it out for you.

[She comes to the couch, peeps into his eye and blows into it. She is in a very suggestive position when Ann steps into the room. Ann is dumb-struck]

There. How's that?

ANDREW: Good. Very good.

ANN: What is this for me at all!

CAROL: *[Swinging around and seeing Ann]* You!

ANN: You? You have the nerve to come to my house messing about with my husband?

ANDREW: What the hell is the matter with you Ann? You going stupid or something?

ANN: *[Almost in hysterics]* I don't what to hear anything
              from you!

ANDREW: What's wrong with you, woman?

ANN: Just leave me alone.

ANDREW: Ann!

ANN: I don't want to hear nothing! *[She exits]*

ANDREW: Ann! What the hell kind of ass is that woman?

CAROL: Is that your wife?

ANDREW: Yes, that's my wife.

CAROL: Are you sure?

ANDREW: Sure, I'm sure. You don't think that by now I'd
              know my own wife?

CAROL: But...but...

ANDREW: But what?

CAROL: No. Forget it. I'm off. Tell Sandra I'll talk to her
              later.

ANDREW: Not at all. What is it? What's the matter?

CAROL: You don't want to hear this.

ANDREW: Sure I do. Come on, tell me what it is. *[Pause]*
              Come on. You can tell me.

CAROL: That's the same woman I was telling you about.

ANDREW: What woman?

CAROL: The one I saw in James' bed!

ANDREW: No. That couldn't be.

CAROL: Yes, I tell you. I saw her with my own eyes.

ANDREW: Are you sure?

CAROL: Absolutely!

ANDREW: *[Thoughtful for a while]* No. You must have been mistaken.

CAROL: Well, I'm glad you think so.

SANDRA: What was that fuss all about? Where's Mommy?

ANDREW: I can't understand what's the matter with your mother. She came and met Carol taking something out of my eye, and obviously thought we were necking. So she raised a god-damn-it and stormed out of the room.

SANDRA: Oh God. Carol I'm really sorry about that. Mommy hasn't been herself these last few weeks so please don't take it badly.

CAROL: Don't worry about it. It's just that she scared the hell out of me. I could almost swear that she is the same woman I was telling you about with James.

SANDRA: Mommy? In James' bed?

CAROL: I think it was her.

SANDRA: Oh no, you must be mistaken. It couldn't possibly have been her.

CAROL: Well, if you say so.

ANDREW: Let me go and ask her.

CAROL: No, don't. I might be wrong and that will only cause more trouble. Let's just forget it.

SANDRA: That's right Dad, because I'm sure there must be
             a mistake. And the state Mommy is in, if you go
             and ask her anything like that, she's only going to
             flare up worse. *[Andrew shrugs]* I'm mixing some
             passionfruit juice. That's okay for you Carol or
             would you prefer something else?

CAROL: That's fine.

SANDRA: How about you, Dad?

ANDREW: I'll drink a glass of it.

SANDRA: Coming up in a minute.

CAROL: I really don't think I ought to stay.

ANDREW: Of course you ought to stay. Everything is going
             to be alright.

             [The door bell rings and Derek enters]

DEREK: Hi. What's happening?

CAROL: Hi, Derek.

DEREK: Where's Sandra?

SANDRA: I'm in the kitchen Derek. Would you like some-
             thing to drink?

DEREK: Not now thanks. *[He sits]*

ANDREW: It looks as if the battle is getting hot.

DEREK: So it seems. *[Sandra comes in and serves drinks
             to Carol and Andrew]*

SANDRA: Well what you think about me getting fired?

DEREK: Somebody is definitely putting some pressure on
             us.

SANDRA: But who would want to do that?

DEREK: Who else? It could only be Daddy.

SANDRA: You think he would really go that far.

DEREK: You don't know him. But I could smell his hand in this. It's funny the way I lost my job just so. And you losing your job now makes it look even fishier. I thought the days of firing pregnant teachers were long over.

SANDRA: Why is life so full of trouble?

ANDREW: The way I see it, you're responsible for all the trouble you're having. All you have to do is get married and your troubles disappear. Of course new ones will arise, but you'll deal with those when they appear.

DEREK: You're the last person I expected that kind of talk from, Andrew. You know we are dead set against the idea of marriage, and I thought you were sympathetic with our views. We can't just run off and get married now.

ANDREW: Why? Afraid of losing face? Too proud to back down? Unable to change your position although common sense says you should? Man, that's a silly attitude that cripples a lot of people.

DEREK: That's the thing that's crippling the whole world. Always the easiest way out. Why doesn't society change! Why doesn't society accept change?

ANDREW: Ah, it does. But it takes ages, generations! You can't afford to wait that long.

DEREK: The change has got to start somewhere.

ANDREW: The way I see it boy, you're crippled before you even start. You don't have any money, you don't have a job, and now Sandra is about to lose her job. You're endangering your future, Sandra's future and the baby's future. Is that what you want to do? *[Long pause]* Look at it this way. *[He rests his hand on Derek's shoulder]* Why don't you get married *[Derek shakes off his hand]*...for the moment. Just for the moment. That'll take the heat off both of you for a while. Sandra will be able to keep her job, and you'd be able to finish school. After you graduate and establish yourself, you can divorce each other and live happily ever after.

SANDRA: Oh Daddy, can't you ever be serious?

ANDREW: But I am serious. I'm very serious.

SANDRA: You make a joke out of everything.

DEREK: Now wait a minute, that's a good idea! As a matter of fact, that's a damn good idea!

ANDREW: Of course it's a good idea.

DEREK: The best.

ANDREW: *[Merrily]* Well, let's fire one on it.

SANDRA: Derek, you really serious?

            [She comes up to Derek, whose attitude has changed to one of playful humor. He embraces her and swings around with her. Then with a mocking bow]

DEREK: Fair damsel, life of my life, leading lady in all my dreams, will you marry me? *[He is about to kiss her hand, but his mood has spread to her, so she pulls it scornfully away]*

SANDRA: Away! Filthy peasant. How dare you think of proposing to a lady of my esteem without a white convertible and a suit of purest silk? *[They all laugh]*

ANDREW: *[Putting an arm around Derek's shoulder]* Me thinks the lady doth protest too much. How sayest thou we slip away to yon Yacht Club for a drink or two?

DEREK: Splendid proposition my dear fellow, splendid.

[Andrew starts leading Derek away. After they have taken two or three steps towards the door, Sandra rushes and puts an arms across Derek's shoulder so he is between herself and Andrew. She is stage right and Andrew is stage left. Their backs are to the audience]

SANDRA: Oh no you don't. *[She swings them around so that all three are facing the audience. She is now stage left and Andrew is stage right]* The two of you are staying right here. Why don't you get some ice from the kitchen and fix drinks for all of us, while I tell Mommy the news. *[She gives them a gentle push]*

DEREK: *[Humorously to Andrew]* You see? She's not even married to me as yet and she's pushing me around already. *[They move towards the kitchen]*

SANDRA: Carol, I hope you know you've got to be one of my bridesmaids.

[Derek and Andrew pause at the kitchen door because of what Sandra has said. They look at each other and shake their heads. Then throwing up their hands in a gesture of resignation, they say as they exit]:
Women, women, women!

CAROL: I'm so happy for you, dear.

SANDRA: I'm so relieved myself. Let me call Mommy. *[Going to the door]* Mommy! Come on out and hear the news. Wait until she hears!

CAROL: Look, I'm going to go give the boys a hand in the kitchen. *[She exits]*

SANDRA: Mommy, come here a minute.

ANN: *[From inside]* What are you annoying me for, child?

SANDRA: Derek and I are going to get married!

ANN: *[Appearing quickly]* What you say?

SANDRA: Derek and I are getting married.

ANN: Oh, thank you Jesus, I know you'd never let me down. *[She embraces Sandra]* Thank you Jesus, thank you. *[Releasing Sandra and breaking contact with Jesus]* So when did you decide?

SANDRA: Just now.

ANN: What a weight has been lifted off me this night. The Lord really hears and answers prayers. Oh give thanks unto the Lord for he is just and his mercies endureth forever. Thank you my Jesus, thank you. You told your father?

SANDRA: Of course.

ANN: What he say?

SANDRA: He's happy.

ANN: And where he gone to now?

SANDRA: In the kitchen.

ANN: Let me get him in here *[She exits, returns immediately, takes hold of Sandra's hand and leads her down right]* What is she still doing here?

SANDRA: That reminds me. How could you let yourself be carried away like that this afternoon, Mommy?

ANN: What you wanted me to do? If I come in and see her...

SANDRA: See what! All she was doing was taking something out of Daddy's eye.

ANN: That's what they tell you. But I saw them with my own two eyes.

SANDRA: Oh, Mommy! You really think she would be kissing Daddy knowing I'd just gone into the kitchen to come back in a minute?

ANN: You were here with them?

SANDRA: Of course I was here. I had just gone into the kitchen to get us something to drink. Daddy came home complaining about something in his eye and I had even tried getting it out myself.

ANN: Well, I didn't realise all of this.

SANDRA: I think you owe her an apology, Mommy.

ANN: Owe her what apology?

SANDRA: Please. She's my good friend and I don't want this to get between us. Okay?

ANN: Well, if you say so.

SANDRA: *[Going to kitchen for Carol]* Carol, come a minute please. *[Carol enters]* Carol, this is my mother. Mommy, Carol Summersdale.

ANN: Hello.

CAROL: Hello.

ANN: This afternoon I was bit upset and...and, I didn't realise...I hope you understand.

CAROL: Oh, don't worry about it. I've forgotten it already.

ANDREW: *[He enters with Derek. They bring on bottles of liquor, some coke and some ginger ale, glasses and a bucket of ice]* The drinks are here.

ANN: Oh Derek, I'm so over-joyed. I always knew that at heart you were a good boy and would do what is right and proper. Has anybody phoned your father to tell him as yet?

DEREK: I hope not. I'm not too anxious for him to hear.

ANN: Why not? I'm going to call him up right now and tell him. *[She is on her way when Andrew calls out]*

ANDREW: Wait a minute Ann. Just wait a minute. Were you over at James' place a few days ago?

ANN: Er...er...yes. I went to find out about the wedding.

ANDREW: Then what the hell were you doing in his bed?

ANN: Well...I...er...

DEREK: I put her there, Andrew. What's the matter with you, getting jealous in your old age? She had one of her dizzy spells and passed out. Dad's room was the closest, so I took her in there to rest for a while.

ANDREW: So that's what happened.

CAROL: That explains it! When I went into the bedroom and saw her there, I put more to it than there really was. Well I guess it's my turn to apologise.

ANN: Let's just cast it aside and forget about it. But you, Andrew! You mean to tell me that your mind is so far in the gutter and so...

SANDRA: Mommy! Just go and make the call please and don't start another quarrel.

ANN: No. You better come with me and make the call, Carol. I'll get supper ready for all of us.

CAROL: That's a good idea. When I'm finished with the call I'll give you a hand. *[They start to exit]*

ANDREW: Hey, Carol, I thought it was all over between you and James.

CAROL: Let's just call this one a close shave, shall we? *[She exits]*

ANDREW: That man has more lives than a cat. *[He pours drinks for Sandra, Derek and himself]* Here's to good luck, good health, happiness and long life!

SANDRA: Here, here.

DEREK: Cheers. *[Derek and Carol speak as they all clink glasses. They drink]*

SANDRA: I hope everything will go smoothly now.

ANDREW: I don't see why it shouldn't.

DEREK: You know, I don't think I want Daddy to be in any way involved with this wedding.

SANDRA: But why?

DEREK: His attitude bugs me.

SANDRA: You're only annoyed because he threw you out the house.

DEREK: It's not only that. He needs to learn that he can't always have things his own way. He can't continue to push his weight around without any regards for other people.

SANDRA: You're just rationalizing Derek. He appears to be coming out on top in this little battle, and that's all that's eating you. You could at least let him win this time, for a change.

DEREK: I'm not rationalizing! Well maybe I am, a little bit.

SANDRA: Of course you are. You can't bear to have him think that he has gotten the best of you.

DEREK: *[On whom the booze is beginning to take slight effect]*You're damn right. Anyway, what the heck! If the wedding is on, I suppose he might as well enjoy it too...while it lasts. Eh, Andrew?

ANDREW: *[Who is also beginning to feel the effects of the drinks]*You sure don't have anything to lose. He's going to be so over-joyed to have you back home, that he'll kill the fatted calf. Hell, he'll kill a dozen fatted calves.

DEREK: Well if he wants to be impressive, he better kill the whole damn herd.

ANDREW: I'll drink to that.

ANN: *[Entering]*How you all mean to tell me that you can plan such an evil, wicked, sinful thing as divorce, before you all even get married!?

ANDREW: For chrissake, Ann...

ANN: And you Andrew, you sit by...

SANDRA: Mommy, just calm down and let me explain everything to you.

ANN: Explain and explain good, because I will not be part of any mockery.

[The door bells rings long and loud]

ANDREW: *[Recognizing the ring]* That has to be James. *[He takes hold of Ann and puts her to sit beside him]* Sit down and keep your mouth shut, Ann.

[The door bell is heard again. Sandra opens it. A beaming James steps in]

JAMES: Congratulations! Congratulations! How's everybody?

SANDRA: Great! We're sort of sitting around waiting for you to get here.

JAMES: *[Giving her a hug]* Ah, you're going to make me a fine daughter-in-law. I came over as soon as I heard the good news. Come on, Molly, take those things into the kitchen and see if you can manage to make yourself useful.

[Molly enters burdened with two huge shopping bags of food stuff and goes into the kitchen]

Nice to know you have come to your senses, my boy. Joe, where the hell are you with the champagne, man.

JOE: *[From outside]* Coming right up, sah. *[Joe enters with a case of Champagne]*

SANDRA: A case of champagne?

JAMES: Well is not every day this boy of mine comes to his senses and gets married to a pretty little girl like you. We got to celebrate the occasion in grand style.

ANDREW: Fine! Fire one in the meantime.

JAMES: Good idea. Pour your father-in-law a scotch and ginger, my dear. Well, Ann, what did I tell you? What did I tell you, Andrew? Didn't I say I would personally see to it that everything works out fine?

ANDREW: How did you manage it?

JAMES: Trade secret, my friend, trade secret. But you know how it is with me. I have my way of handling these ticklish little problems. When I make a promise, I make a debt. And after all, never let it be said that I, James Llewellyn Wellington, ever made a debt that I didn't honor.

DEREK: Go ahead and gloat, Daddy, gloat your head off.

JAMES: What the devil are you talking about?

DEREK: You know damn well what I'm talking about. I'm talking about you turning the screws on me. I'm talking about you getting me fired and blocking me from getting hired anyplace else. And no doubt you had a little chat with the school board and had Sandra fired too. Jesus Christ Daddy!

JAMES: Don't let it upset you son. Things are going to work out just fine. *[Offering his hand]* No hard feelings.

DEREK: *[Slapping the hand away]* Like hell no hard feelings!

SANDRA: *[Intercepting with a drink]* Please, please! No more quarreling, please.

JAMES: *[Taking a drink]* You're quite right my dear. We've had enough of those, the two of us. Listen Derek, let's reason this thing out. Getting married isn't going to hurt you. You're going to have a nice wife, who I'll arrange to have transferred to Jamaica so she can be with you while you finish school. But if you had gone to live in sin, you would be asking me to change my values of what is right and what is wrong.

DEREK: *[With an ironical sneer]* Your values of what is right and what is wrong.

JAMES: I know you young people have your own modern ideas of how to live life, and I'm not saying that you all are wrong. But after all, I'm an old man now, and it's easier to destroy old men than to change them. And if you had gone and done what you were planning, you would not only be destroying me, but yourself and Sandra, and the reputation of the whole Forgerty family.

DEREK: Amen, brother, amen! You may be able to con the rest of the world, Dad, but I know well enough that the only criterion you have of right and wrong, is what brings you votes and what doesn't.

JAMES: Surprise at you my boy, surprise at you. Don't be giving away my trade secrets like that in public. Well, what the hell. We're all one big family now, so there should be no secrets between us anyway. And take it from me, Derek, by getting married to Sandra, you're doing absolutely the right thing.

DEREK: One of these days, Dad, one of these days... *[They embrace]*

JAMES: Come on, give us some music somebody. We have an engagement to celebrate. Ann, how come you're so glum. Cheer up. Call up some friends and let's get this celebration going.

ANN: *[Getting up]* No. My conscience couldn't let me go through with it. Oh, Mr. Wellington, this is only a sinful, wicked, evil trick.

JAMES: What the devil are you talking about?

ANN: They are planning to divorce one another as soon as Derek gets out of school.

SANDRA: Mommy, for heaven's sake, don't be so silly. After all the trouble we've been through, you think we'd want to go through it all again with a divorce? The mere thoughts of how you and James are going to carry on, is enough to change even the devil's mind. Besides, divorces are so expensive that I'm sure it's not going to be worth it.

ANN: Don't listen to her, Mr. Wellington! They have it all figured out.

JAMES: Anything go like this?

ANDREW: Come, come. Let's not cross our bridges before we get to them.

JAMES: Well said, well said. We'll deal with that when and if the time comes. Right now we have the engagement and then the wedding. *[To Sandra]* Try out the marriage business for yourself and see what it's like. If you don't like it, then…*[He completes the statement with a gesture of his hand]* But, before you go and do anything stupid, see to it that you give me some healthy grandchildren. Legitimate ones too.

SANDRA: Just see to it that you don't get yourself destroyed too soon.

JAMES: *[Laughing]* Don't worry about that. Your old father-in-law is harder to sink than a battle ship. *[Calling]* Where's the champagne! *[Molly enters from kitchen with glasses of champagne on a tray. She serves each person. When she gets to Ann, Ann hesitates]*

ANDREW: Go on, Ann. Have one for the stomachs sake.

ANN: Well, I suppose I might as well. *[She takes a drink and downs it]* For the stomach's sake.

JAMES: Joe, get in here and have some champagne. Have a glass too, Molly. *[Joe enters]* Where's the music around here?

[Sandra puts on some hot calypso music. At the same time, Carol enters from the kitchen with a tray of hors d'oeuvres. James takes the tray from her, puts it on the centre table and they start to dance. Derek and Sandra dance. Molly and Joe dance. By and by, Andrew and Ann do a jig. They all continue to dance as the lights fade out]

THE END